汽车专业英语

（第 3 版）

主　编　吴金顺　常同珍
副主编　杨　艳　张　鹏
　　　　李洪亮　杨　冲

北京理工大学出版社
BEIJING INSTITUTE OF TECHNOLOGY PRESS

内 容 简 介

本书根据吴金顺、常同珍主编的《汽车专业英语（第2版）》修订而成。全书教学资源包括纸质版教材、信息化资源、二维码资源和音频资源4部分。其中，纸质版教材分为汽车运用与维修篇、汽车营销与服务篇、汽车美容与装饰篇和汽车英语电器综合实训篇4大部分内容，包含21个任务和实训教学。除个别任务外，各教学任务由课文正文、图解、词汇学习、课堂互动、语法分析、课文注释、安全提示、课后练习、课文译文和练习答案组成。

本书新增了5课新能源汽车、宝马服务、营销与服务等全新内容；充实了汽车英语电器综合实训篇教学内容；新增了电子白板游戏课件等信息化资源；新增了互动课堂；更新了原书课文内容，可以更好地实施"教""学""做"一体化教学，有助于高等院校汽车专业的学生掌握汽车的结构原理、性能、拆装、检测、故障诊断与排除、维修、营销与服务、装饰与美容等英文运用能力方面的知识。

本书涵盖面更广，图文并茂，信息量大，适合作为高等院校汽车专业的专业英语教材使用，也可供汽车行业相关从业人员及广大汽车使用者参考。

版权专有　侵权必究

图书在版编目（CIP）数据

汽车专业英语/吴金顺，常同珍主编. —3 版. —北京：北京理工大学出版社，2019.12　（2022.7重印）

ISBN 978-7-5640-6196-8

Ⅰ. ①汽… Ⅱ. ①吴… ②常… Ⅲ. ①汽车工程－英语－高等学校－教材　Ⅳ. ①U46

中国版本图书馆 CIP 数据核字（2019）第 290017 号

出版发行　/　北京理工大学出版社有限责任公司
社　　址　/　北京市海淀区中关村南大街5号
邮　　编　/　100081
电　　话　/　(010)68914775（总编室）
　　　　　　　(010)82562903（教材售后服务热线）
　　　　　　　(010)68944723（其他图书服务热线）
网　　址　/　http://www.bitpress.com.cn
经　　销　/　全国各地新华书店
印　　刷　/　唐山富达印务有限公司
开　　本　/　710 毫米 × 1000 毫米　1/16
印　　张　/　14　　　　　　　　　　　　　　　责任编辑　/　梁铜华
字　　数　/　266 千字　　　　　　　　　　　　文案编辑　/　梁铜华
版　　次　/　2019 年 12 月第 3 版　2022 年 7 月第 3 次印刷　责任校对　/　周瑞红
定　　价　/　42.00 元　　　　　　　　　　　　责任印制　/　李志强

图书出现印装质量问题，请拨打售后服务热线，本社负责调换

前 言

为全面贯彻落实党的教育方针,突出职业教育的类型特点,深化职业教育"三教"改革,强化知识传授与技术技能培养并重,强化学生职业素养的养成和专业技术的积累,满足社会对高素质技术技能人才英文运用能力的要求,我们以国家新能源汽车高水平专业群建设为契机,结合高职发展的新要求、校企"双元"合作开发,对教材《汽车专业英语(第2版)》进行了修订。

本教材根据高等职业教育的培养目标编写,是对吴金顺、常同珍主编的教材《汽车专业英语(第2版)》的修订。本教材的教学资源包括纸质版教材、信息化资源、二维码资源和音频资源4部分。其中,纸质版教材分为汽车运用与维修篇、汽车营销与服务篇、汽车美容与装饰篇、汽车英语电器综合实训篇4大部分内容,包含21个任务和实训教学。每个任务基本由课文正文、图解、词汇学习、课堂互动、语法注释、课文注释、安全提示、课后练习、课文译文和练习答案等内容组成。本次修订新增了5课新能源汽车、宝马服务、营销与服务等全新内容;充实了汽车英语电器综合实训篇教学内容;新增了信息化教学资源(电子白板游戏课件、译文及练习答案二维码、信息化教学的教案、建议教学时数、音频资源等);新增了互动课堂;更新了原教材课文内容,可以更好地实施"教""学""做"一体化教学。

本教材编委均为国家高水平专业群(湖北交通职业技术学院新能源汽车专业群)建设团队的骨干教师和企业专家,第一主编曾留学美国和加拿大5年;副主编之一担任宝马武汉培训基地项目主管,获得宝马校企合作项目2015年度非技术培训师最佳贡献奖、宝马校企合作项目五年杰出贡献奖,同时是丰田技术员培训教师。

本教材采用项目化教学,分模块编辑,以典型工作任务等为载体组织各教学单元的学习,坚持育训结合,涵盖企业生产案例、操作流程、任务工单、岗位标准等内容;信息化教学资源丰富,配套开发了电子白板教学资源、二维码教学资源(课文译文和练习答案)、信息化电子教案、多媒体课件、教学图片、单元教学设计、同步习题及答案等信息化教学资源。综合实训篇融入了作者对该课程实施教学改革的成果,以推进理实一体化教材、教法改革。英文词汇学习方法、翻译技巧的培养、各种有趣的课堂活动均能激发学生的学习兴趣,易学易懂。本教材有助于高职高专院校汽车类专业的学生提升汽车的结构原理、性能、拆装、检测、故障诊断与排除、维修、营销与服务、装饰与美容等方面的英文运用能力,也可供汽车行业相关从业人员和广大的汽车使用者参考使用，满足职业教育对外开放和国际合作的需要，对我国汽车产业的国际化发展及"一带一路"发展具有很好的促进作用。

本教材体现了"Teaching、Training、Testing"3T教学法的特色与创新；看图识字、卡片识别、交互式电子白板游戏课件等是新增课堂活动的亮点；大部分任务中的"安全提示"体现了职业素养教育；以二维码形式呈现的课文译文和练习答案有助于老师教、学生学。这些都方便了老师备课、组织互动活动及活跃课堂气氛，适合现阶段高职高专院校的实际情况。

本教材涵盖面更广，图文并茂，信息量大，是一部结构合理、内容丰富且实用性强的教材。建议教学时数：PartⅠ50学时，PartⅡ14学时，PartⅢ12学时，PartⅣ6~8学时。

本书由湖北交通职业技术学院吴金顺、常同珍主编。其中，吴金顺负责全书资源整体设计和统稿，编写Task1、Task5、Task6、Task10、Task14、Task15、Task16、综合实训篇及所有信息化资源的制作；常同珍负责全书内容的策划，编写Task8、Task13、Task19、Task20、Task21。副主编杨艳编写Task4、Task7、Task12，张鹏编写Task2、Task3，李洪亮编写Task17、Task18，杨冲编写Task9、Task11。

感谢曾喜红先生（首批湖北省售后服务协会的技术专家、武汉交通广播电台FM89.6电台"汽车大管家"特聘解读专家）对本书编写给予的大力支持和帮助，感谢李雄、邬玉琴、陈雪、屈艺、江舸、杨朝、黄军提出的宝贵意见；同时也感谢北京理工大学出版社给予我们的支持和鼓励；感谢各级领导、作者家人和朋友们给予我们的理解和支持。编者在编写过程中，直接或间接地引用了一些学者的研究成果，在此表示衷心的感谢。

由于编写时间紧迫，水平有限，书中难免有不妥之处，欢迎读者提出宝贵意见。

编 者

目录

Part I Automobile Application and Services
汽车运用与维修篇

Task 1　English Abbreviations for Automobiles …………………… (3)
　　常用汽车英文缩略词 …………………………………………… (3)
　　Classroom Activities 课堂活动 ………………………………… (6)

Task 2　Basic Structure of Automobiles ……………………………… (7)
　　汽车基本结构 …………………………………………………… (7)
　　Classroom Activities 课堂活动 ………………………………… (10)
　　Safety Tips 安全提示 …………………………………………… (11)
　　Exercises 练习 …………………………………………………… (12)

Task 3　Overview of New Energy Vehicles ………………………… (13)
　　新能源汽车概述 ………………………………………………… (13)
　　Classroom Activities 课堂活动 ………………………………… (17)
　　Exercises 练习 …………………………………………………… (18)

Task 4　Vehicle Information Displaying System and Services ……… (20)
　　汽车信息显示系统及检修 ……………………………………… (20)
　　Classroom Activities 课堂活动 ………………………………… (26)
　　Safety Tips 安全提示 …………………………………………… (27)
　　Exercises 练习 …………………………………………………… (27)

Task 5　EFI System Operating Principle and DTC Identification …… (30)
　　电子燃油喷射系统工作原理及故障诊断代码识别 …………… (30)
　　Classroom Activities 课堂活动 ………………………………… (36)
　　Safety Tips 安全提示 …………………………………………… (37)
　　Exercises 练习 …………………………………………………… (37)

Task 6　Cooling System Service Manual …………………………… (40)
　　冷却系统维修手册 ……………………………………………… (40)
　　Classroom Activities 课堂活动 ………………………………… (44)
　　Safety Tips 安全提示 …………………………………………… (46)
　　Exercises 练习 …………………………………………………… (46)

Task 7　Ignition System Service Manual …………………………… (50)
　　点火系统维修手册 ……………………………………………… (50)
　　Classroom Activities 课堂活动 ………………………………… (55)
　　Safety Tips 安全提示 …………………………………………… (56)
　　Exercises 练习 …………………………………………………… (57)

Task 8　Starting System Service Procedures ………………………… (60)
　　起动系统检测维修 ……………………………………………… (60)
　　Classroom Activities 课堂活动 ………………………………… (65)
　　Safety Tips 安全提示 …………………………………………… (66)
　　Exercises 练习 …………………………………………………… (67)

Task 9　Valvetronic Principles (BMW Service) …………………… (69)
　　电子气门原理（宝马服务）…………………………………… (69)
　　Classroom Activities 课堂活动 ………………………………… (71)
　　Safety Tips 安全提示 …………………………………………… (72)
　　Exercises 练习 …………………………………………………… (72)

Task 10　Automatic Transmission and Troubleshooting …………… (73)
　　自动变速箱及其故障排除 ……………………………………… (73)
　　Classroom Activities 课堂活动 ………………………………… (78)
　　Safety Tips 安全提示 …………………………………………… (79)
　　Exercises 练习 …………………………………………………… (80)

Task 11　Brake System Service Manual ……………………………… (82)
　　制动系统维修手册 ……………………………………………… (82)
　　Classroom Activities 课堂活动 ………………………………… (91)
　　Safety Tips 安全提示 …………………………………………… (92)
　　Exercises 练习 …………………………………………………… (92)

Task 12　Power Steering System Services …………………………… (96)
　　动力转向系统检测维修 ………………………………………… (96)
　　Classroom Activities 课堂活动 ………………………………… (103)
　　Safety Tips 安全提示 …………………………………………… (104)
　　Exercises 练习 …………………………………………………… (104)

Task 13　Air Conditioning System Services ………………………… (107)
　　空调系统检测维修 ……………………………………………… (107)
　　Classroom Activities 课堂活动 ………………………………… (112)
　　Safety Tips 安全提示 …………………………………………… (113)
　　Exercises 练习 …………………………………………………… (114)

Task 14　Lighting System Service Manual ···············(117)
　　照明系统维修手册 ·······································(117)
　　Classroom Activities 课堂活动 ·························(122)
　　Safety Tips 安全提示 ··································(123)
　　Exercises 练习 ··(123)

Part II　Automobile Marketing and Services
汽车营销与服务篇

Task 15　Automobile Trading
　　汽车交易 ··(129)
　　Exercises 练习 ··(139)

Task 16　Orders and Contracts
　　订单与合同 ··(140)
　　Safety Tips 安全提示 ··································(146)
　　Exercises 练习 ··(146)

Task 17　Automobile E-commerce
　　汽车电子商务 ··(147)
　　Exercises 练习 ··(150)

Task 18　Auto Insurance
　　汽车保险 ··(152)
　　Exercises 练习 ··(156)

Part III　Auto Beauty and Decoration
汽车美容与装饰篇

Task 19　Auto Body
　　汽车车身 ··(161)
　　Safety Tips 安全提示 ··································(167)
　　Exercises 练习 ··(167)

Task 20　Car Care
　　汽车美容 ··(169)
　　Safety Tips 安全提示 ··································(179)
　　Exercises 练习 ··(179)

Task 21　Automobile Decoration
　　汽车装饰 ··(182)
　　Safety Tips 安全提示 ··································(193)
　　Exercises 练习 ··(193)

Part IV 汽车英语电器综合实训篇

一、汽车全车线路实训台介绍 …………………………………………（199）
二、各系统部件名称中英文介绍 ………………………………………（202）
三、电器综合实训教学组织与案例 ……………………………………（208）
四、电器实训学习工单 …………………………………………………（210）
五、专业词汇拓展训练工单 ……………………………………………（213）

参考文献 ……………………………………………………………………（216）

Part I

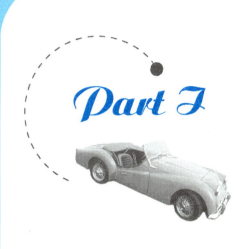

Automobile Application and Services

汽车运用与维修篇

Task 1

English Abbreviations for Automobiles
常用汽车英文缩略词

学习目标:
1. 了解常用的英文汽车专业缩略词;
2. 熟悉英文汽车专业缩略词的拼写规律及中文含义;
3. 能读懂汽车技术资料中的缩略词。

Abbreviation	English Meaning	Chinese Meaning
1. A/C	Air Conditioning	空调
2. A/F	Air Fuel Ratio	空燃比
3. A/T	Automatic Transmission	自动变速器
4. AB	Air Bag	气囊
5. ABS	Anti-lock Brake System	防抱死制动系统
6. ABS	Anti-skid Brake System	防滑制动系统
7. AC	Automatic Control	自动控制
8. ACC	Accessory	附属设备
9. ACL	Air Cleaner	空气滤清器
10. ACTS	Air Charge Temperature Sensor	进气温度传感器
11. ADM	Advance Module	点火提前角控制模块
12. AEC	Automotive Emission Control	汽车排放控制
13. AFS	Air Flow Sensor	空气流量传感器
14. ALT	Alternator	交流发电机
15. APP	Accelerator Pedal Position	加速器踏板位置
16. APS	Absolute Pressure Sensor	绝对压力传感器
17. ASSY	Assembly	总成
18. ATA	Anti-theft Alarm	防盗报警
19. ATF	Automatic Transmission Fluid	自动变速器油液

Abbreviation	English Meaning	Chinese Meaning
20. AWD	All Wheel Drive	全轮驱动
21. AWS	All Wheel Steering	全轮转向
22. B+	Battery Positive Voltage	蓄电池正极电压
23. BAS	Brake Assisted System	制动助力系统
24. BAT	Battery	蓄电池
25. BCM	Body Control Module	车身控制模块
26. BEV	Battery Electric Vehicle	纯电动汽车
27. BLS	Back-up Light Switch	倒车灯开关
28. BMW	Bavarian Motor Works	德国宝马汽车公司
29. CB	Circuit Breaker	断路器
30. CCM	Central Control Module	中央控制模块
31. CFI	Central Fuel Injection	中央燃油喷射
32. CFI	Continuous Fuel Injection	连续燃油喷射
33. CID	Cylinder Identification	气缸识别
34. CIL	Clear Indicating Light	消除（其故障码）指示灯
35. CPP	Clutch Pedal Position	离合器踏板位置
36. CPS	Camshaft Position Sensor	凸轮轴位置传感器
37. CPS	Crankshaft Position Sensor	曲轴位置传感器
38. CPU	Central Processing Unit	中央处理单元
39. CRS	Child Restraint System	儿童安全保护系统
40. CSI	Cold Start Injector	冷起动喷油器
41. CTP	Closed Throttle Position	节气门关闭位置
42. CTS	Coolant Temperature Sensor	冷却液温度传感器
43. CVT	Continuously Variable Transmission	无级变速器
44. DFI	Direct Fuel Injection	直接燃油喷射
45. DID	Direct Injection Diesel	柴油直接喷射
46. DLC	Data Link Connector	诊断传输接头
47. DMM	Digital Multimeter	数字式万用表
48. DOHC	Double Overhead Camshaft	顶置双凸轮轴
49. DTC	Diagnostic Trouble Code	诊断故障代码
50. ECA	Electronic Control Assembly	电子控制总成
51. ECM	Engine Control Module	发动机控制模块
52. ECT	Electronic Control Transmission	电控变速器
53. ECU	Electronic Control Unit	电子控制单元

Task 1　English Abbreviations for Automobiles

Abbreviation	English Meaning	Chinese Meaning
54. EFI	Electronic Fuel Injection	电子燃油喷射
55. EGR	Exhaust Gas Recirculation	废气再循环
56. EIN	Engine Identification Number	发动机识别号码
57. FCFV	Fuel Cell Electric Vehicle	燃料电池电动汽车
58. FR	Front Right	右前
59. FWD	Front Wheel Drive	前轮驱动
60. GND	Ground	搭铁
61. GPS	Global Position System	全球定位系统
62. HARN	Harness	线束,配线
63. HEV	Hybrid Electric Vehicle	混合动力电动汽车
64. HHT	Hand-held Tester	手持式检测仪
65. IACV	Idle Air Control Valve	怠速空气控制阀
66. IATS	Intake Air Temperature Sensor	进气温度传感器
67. ID	Identification	辨认,识别
68. ISC	Idle Speed Control	怠速速度控制
69. ISO	International Standard Organization	国际标准组织
70. KS	Knock Sensor	爆震传感器
71. L4	In-line Four Cylinder (Engine)	直列式四气缸(发动机)
72. LED	Light Emitting Diode	发光二极管
73. LEV	Low Emission Vehicle	低排放汽车
74. M/T	Manual Transmission	手动变速箱
75. MAFS	Mass Air Flow Sensor	质量型空气流量传感器
76. MAPS	Manifold Absolute Pressure Sensor	歧管绝对压力传感器
77. MIL	Malfunction Indicator Lamp	故障指示灯
78. MPI	Multi-point Fuel Injection	多点燃油喷射
79. NEV	New Energy Vehicle	新能源汽车
80. OBD II	On-board Diagnostic II	第二代车载诊断系统
81. OEM	Original Equipment Manufacturer	原装设备生产厂
82. OSHA	Occupational Safety and Health Act	职业安全与卫生条例
83. P/W	Power Window	电动车窗
84. PCM	Power Control Module	动力控制模块
85. PCV	Positive Crankcase Ventilation	曲轴箱强制通风
86. PFI	Port Fuel Injection	进气口燃油喷射
87. P	Park	停车
88. RAR	Repair as Required	视情修理
89. RHD	Right Handle Drive	右侧驾驶

Abbreviation	English Meaning	Chinese Meaning
90. RM	Relay Module	继电器模块
91. RPM	Revolution per Minute	转/分
92. RR	Rear Right	右后
93. RWD	Rear Wheel Drive	后轮驱动
94. S/R	Sun Roof	遮阳板
95. SAE	Society of Automotive Engineers	美国汽车工程师学会
96. SPEC	Specification	规格
97. SPI	Single-point Fuel Injection	单点燃油喷射
98. 4S	Sale, Spare, Service, Survey	汽车销售、配件供应、维修服务、技术信息反馈(4S店)
99. T/N	Tool Number	工具编号
100. TB	Throttle Body	节气门体
101. TBI	Throttle Body Injection	节气门体喷射
102. TC	Turbocharger	涡轮增压器
103. TCC	Torque Converter Clutch	液力变矩器离合器
104. TDCL	Test Diagnostic Communication Link	自诊接头
105. TPS	Throttle Position Sensor	节气门位置传感器
106. TSB	Technical Service Bulletin	技术维修通报
107. VIN	Vehicle Identification Number	车辆识别号码
108. VSS	Vehicle Speed Sensor	车速传感器
109. VSV	Vacuum Solenoid Valve	真空电磁阀
110. VVLS	Variable Valve Lift System	可变气门升程机构
111. VVTS	Variable Valve Timing System	可变气门正时系统
112. WOT	Wide Open Throttle	节气门全开
113. WSS	Wheel Speed Sensor	车轮速度传感器
114. ZEV	Zero Emission Vehicle	零排放汽车

Classroom Activities 课堂活动

Image-matching activity（图片与英文词汇匹配活动）：应用交互式电子白板互动课堂工具，设计学习游戏，让学生在游戏中训练词汇。移动英文单词或词组到相应图片的框内。完成一组训练后点击Check键，可检测对错（游戏操作方法及截屏说明放在信息化教学教案里；动态的游戏课件与教案一起，均放在信息化教学资源文件夹里）。

Task 2

Basic Structure of Automobiles
汽车基本结构

学习目标：
1. 掌握汽车四大组成部分的专业英文词汇；
2. 了解汽车各结构的功能及组成。

 Text 课文

 Introduction

Today's automobiles are made up of many devices and mechanisms. The basic structure of automobiles of different models, types and those produced by different manufacturers contains four sections of engine, chassis, body and electrical equipment. See Figure 2 – 1.

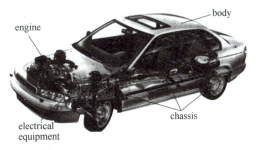

Figure 2 – 1 Basic structure of automobiles

1. Engine

The engine is called the "heart" of automobiles, and supplies the power to move the vehicle. Reciprocating piston type of internal combustion engines are widely used in modern automobiles. They produce pressure through combustion and expansion of mixed inflammable gas in cylinder, push forward the movement of piston and release power through revolving bent axles. Gasoline engines are mainly made up of two major mechanisms and five major systems. Two major settings refer to crank connecting rod mechanism and valve timing mechanism. These systems refer to fuel system, ignition system, cooling system, lubricating system and starting system. See Figure 2 – 2.

Figure 2 – 2 Engine assembly (2.4 Liter V6-Motor)

2. Chassis

The chassis is mainly used to receive power from the engine. It is able to cause movement in automobiles and ensures the normal driving of automobiles according to the control of drivers. Chassis is made up of transmission system, suspension system, steering system and brake system. See Figure 2 – 3.

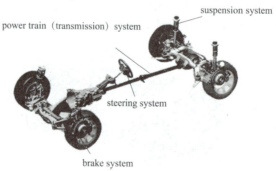

Figure 2 – 3 Chassis assembly

3. Body

The body is installed on the frame of chassis. It is where drivers work and passengers or goods are carried. The body shall provide drivers with convenient operation condition and provide passengers with safe and comfortable environment or ensure the perfect condition of

Task 2 Basic Structure of Automobiles

goods. Typical body of trucks shall include front plate production, cab and compartment among other components. Other special vehicles also have some special equipment. Besides, body shall also include doors, windows, car locks, internal and external decorations, accessories, seats and various front sheet metal parts in cars. The body of an automobile makes it extremely attractive with brilliant colors and modernized appearance. See Figure 2-4.

Figure 2-4 Body frame assembly

4. Electrical Equipment

The electrical equipment consists of power supply system, engine starting system and ignition system, automobile lighting and signal system. Besides, various electronic systems are widely applied to modern automobiles such as micro-computers, CPU and various artificial intelligence devices, conspicuously improving the performance of automobiles. See Figure 2-5.

Figure 2-5 Electrical equipment

New Words 生词

1. automobile [ˈɔtəmə‚bil] n. 汽车
2. engine [ˈendʒɪn] n. 引擎，发动机
3. structure [ˈstrʌktʃər] n. 结构；构造
4. chassis [ˈʃæsi] n. 底盘，底架
5. body [ˈbɑːdi] n. 身体；车身
6. cylinder [ˈsɪlɪndər] n. 圆筒；气缸
7. gasoline [gæsəˈliːn] n. 汽油
8. diesel [ˈdiːzl] n. 柴油机；柴油
9. ignition [ɪgˈnɪʃn] n. 点火，点燃
10. transmission [trænzˈmɪʃn, trænsˈmɪʃn] n. 传动装置，[机] 变速器
11. passenger [ˈpæsndʒər] n. 旅客；乘客
12. transaxle [trænsˈæksəl] n. 变速驱动桥
13. brake [breɪk] n. 刹车；制动
14. clutch [klʌtʃ] v. 紧握 n. 离合器
15. wheel [wiːl] n. 车轮；方向盘；转动

Phrases and Expressions 短语与表达

1. power train   动力传动系统
2. transmission system   传动系统
3. suspension system   悬挂系统
4. brake system   制动系统
5. steering system   转向系统
6. micro-computer   微型计算机
7. be made up of   由……组成
8. fuel system   燃油系统
9. starting system   起动系统

Classroom Activities 课堂活动

1. Translate the English words in Figure 2–1, Figure 2–3 into Chinese, and share with classmates. (将图 2–1、图 2–3 中的英文单词翻译成中文，并与同学们分享。)

2. Image-matching activity（图片与英文单词匹配活动）：应用交互式电子白板互动课堂工具，设计学习游戏，让学生在游戏中训练词汇。移动英文单词或词组到相应图片的框内，完成一组训练后单击 Check 键，可检测对错(游戏操作方法及截屏说明放在信息化教学教案里；动态的游戏课件与教案一起均放在信息化教学资源文件夹里)。

Task 2 Basic Structure of Automobiles

Text Notes 课文注释

1. Today's automobiles are made up of many devices and mechanisms. The basic structure of automobiles of different models, types and those produced by different manufacturers contains four sections of engine, chassis, body and electrical equipment.
   现代汽车是由多个装置和机构组成的。不同型号、不同类型及不同厂家生产的汽车,其基本结构都是由发动机、底盘、车身和电气设备四大部分组成的。

2. The engine is called the "heart" of automobiles, and supplies the power to move the vehicle.
   发动机被称为汽车的"心脏",为汽车提供动力使其移动。

3. The chassis is mainly used to receive power from the engine. It is able to cause movement in automobiles and ensures the normal driving of automobiles according to the control of drivers. Chassis is made up of transmission system, suspension system, steering system and brake system.
   底盘主要用来接收发动机的动力,能使汽车产生运动,并保证汽车按照驾驶员的操纵正常行驶。底盘由传动系统、悬挂系统、转向系统和制动系统组成。

4. The body is installed on the frame of chassis. It is where drivers work and passengers or goods are carried. The body shall provide drivers with convenient operation condition and provide passengers with safe and comfortable environment or ensure the perfect condition of goods.
   车身安装在汽车底盘的车架上,它是驾驶员工作的场所,也是容纳乘客或货物的场所。车身应为驾驶员提供方便的操作条件,为乘客提供安全舒适的环境或保证货物完好无损。

Safety Tips 安全提示

使用手动工具的安全提示:
1. 为了更好地控制和安全起见,拉动扳手的方向要始终朝你自己,切勿推动扳手。
2. 所有扳手和手动工具应保持清洁、防止生锈,以便更好地使用。
3. 要始终使用六角套筒或套筒扳手拧紧和松开螺栓或螺母。
4. 当需要较大的紧固力矩时使用套筒扳手,需要提高速度时使用开口扳手。
5. 在扳手或棘轮手柄上切勿使用加长套筒或其他类型的"加长手柄"。若需要更大的紧固力矩,则需要使用更大的工具。可使用加注润滑油或给紧固件加热的方法进行拆卸,通过加热方式拆下的螺栓或螺母必须被更换。
6. 在需要用专用工具的场合,务必使用合适的专用工具。
7. 切勿将工具暴露在过热环境中,高温会降低金属强度。

xercises 练习

Part I Answer the questions according to the text.

1) What are the four basic sections of an automobile?
2) What's the function of the engine?
3) What consist of a chassis?

Part II Match the following English phrases in Column A with the equivalents in Column B.

A	B
1. Battery	To reduce the speed of a brake
2. Parking	To set into motion, operation, or activity
3. Braking	A single cell, such as a dry cell, that produces electricity
4. Transmission	To put or leave for a time in a certain location
5. Start	An automotive assembly of gears by which power is transmitted from the engine to a driving axle

Part III Translate the following into English or Chinese.

1) 柴油机
2) 底盘
3) 离合器
4) 制动系统
5) suspension system
6) steering system
7) ignition system
8) electrical equipment

Part IV Translate the following sentences into English.

1) 汽车的构造基本上是一样的。
2) 发动机是为汽车提供动力的设备。
3) 任何汽车都由发动机、底盘、车身以及电气设备四部分组成。

译文答案

发音训练

Task 3

Overview of New Energy Vehicles
新能源汽车概述

学习目标：
1. 了解新能源汽车的定义及分类；
2. 了解混合动力电动汽车、纯电动汽车、燃料电池电动汽车、天然气汽车、其他新能源汽车的概念及特点。

Introduction

New energy vehicles refer to vehicles that adopt unconventional vehicle fuels as power sources (or use conventional fuels but adopt new vehicle power devices), integrate advanced technologies in vehicle power control and drive, and form advanced technical principles, new technologies and new structures. See Figure 3–1. New energy vehicles are an important way to solve the problem of energy shortage and environmental pollution, and they have become the development of automobile industry in the 21st century. New energy vehicles mainly include hybrid electric vehicle (HEV), battery electric vehicle (BEV), fuel cell electric vehicle (FCEV), natural gas vehicle and other new energy vehicles.

Figure 3–1 New energy vehicles

1. Hybrid Electric Vehicle (HEV)

A hybrid electric vehicle is a hybrid-type electric vehicle powered by more than one energy converter, that is, an electric vehicle using a battery and a secondary energy unit. See Figure 3-2. At present, hybrid electric vehicles mostly apply the mixed mode of the traditional fuel engine and electric power. Its key technology is hybrid power system, the key technique is hybrid power system, which directly affects the performance of the whole vehicle.

The advantage of hybrid electric vehicle is that the maximum power of internal combustion engine can be determined by the average required power, so that the internal combustion engine can work under the optimal working condition of low fuel consumption and little pollution, which can usually reduce emissions. The batteries used in the hybrid electric vehicles can recover energy from braking and other conditions. At the same time, the hybrid electric vehicles also have the problems such as the high price, small driving range and relatively insufficient power.

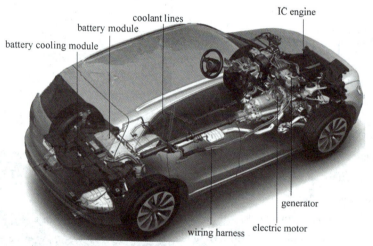

Figure 3-2 Hybrid electric vehicle

2. Battery Electric Vehicle (BEV)

A battery electric vehicle is a vehicle which is powered by the vehicle power supply, and the wheel travels is driven by motor, and which meets the requirements of the road traffic and safety regulations. See Figure 3-3. Battery electric vehicles are completely driven by the rechargeable batteries, and the key components are the motors and batteries, while the difficulty limited for the application of battery electric vehicles lies in the power storage technology.

Task 3　Overview of New Energy Vehicles 　　15

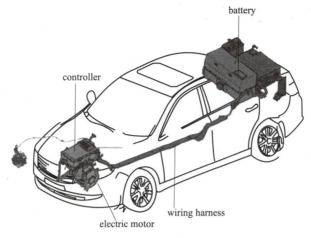

Figure 3 – 3　Battery electric vehicle

The battery electric vehicle has a wide application prospect, and has the advantages with no pollution, low noise and high energy efficiency. However, the energy stored by the battery per unit weight is too small, and the driving range after charging is not ideal. At present, the development of electric vehicle industry must reconstruct the supporting infrastructure network (the charging stations), which requires a large amount of investment.

3. Fuel Cell Electric Vehicle (FCEV)

A fuel cell electric vehicle is a new type of vehicle that uses hydrogen and methanol as fuel to generate an electric current through the chemical reactions, and is powered by an electric motor. Compared with internal combustion engines, the fuel cell electric vehicles convert the chemical energy directly into the electricity energy through the battery, and which use the electric motors to drive, but don't use the combustion process of the fuel. Their energy conversion efficiency is 2 – 3 times higher than that of the internal combustion engines. See Figure 3 – 4.

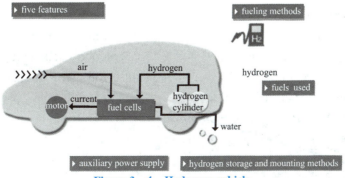

Figure 3 – 4　Hydrogen vehicle

Fuel cell chemical reaction process does not produce pollutants, and has low noise. However, the production, integration and industrialization of fuel cells stack are still to be developed.

4. Natural Gas Vehicle

Natural gas vehicles are the vehicles that use natural gas as fuel, also known as "blue power" vehicles. According to the chemical composition and form of natural gas, it can be divided into the compressed natural gas (CNG), liquefied natural gas (LNG) and liquefied petroleum gas (LPG).

Natural gas fuel has the advantages with low pollution, low cost, high safety performance, but with low power performance, inconvenient storage and transportation. By considering the large-scale application, it is necessary to build the corresponding gas filling station and the transportation pipeline of natural gas for the gas filling station, and it has greater cost. At present, the natural gas vehicles in China are mostly used in the public transportation field.

5. Other New Energy Vehicles

In addition to the above new energy vehicles, alcohol and ether fuel are also used in the new energy vehicles. For example, the fuel used in ethanol cars is ethanol gasoline, and the vehicles are relatively mature at present. Dimethyl ether automobiles apply dimethyl ether as the fuel of compression combustion engine, which has been applied successfully in dimethyl ether city bus in China.

New Words 生词

1. conventional ['kən'venʃənl] adj. 传统的;常见的
2. shortage ['ʃɔːrtɪdʒ] n. 缺乏;不足
3. integrate ['ɪntɪɡreɪt] adj. 整合的;集成体
4. environment [ɪn'vaɪrənmənt] n. 环境,外界
5. emission [ɪ'mɪʃn] n. (光、热等的) 发射,散发;排放
6. industry ['ɪndəstri] n. 产业;工业
7. hybrid ['haɪbrɪd] n. 混合物 adj. 混合的

8. module ['mɑːdʒuːl] n. [计] 模块;组件
9. cell [sel] n. 细胞;电池
10. coolant ['kuːlənt] n. 冷却剂
11. pollution [pə'luːʃn] n. 污染;污染物
12. controller [kən'troʊlər] n. 控制器
13. alcohol ['ælkəhɔːl] n. 酒精,乙醇
14. hydrogen ['haɪdrədʒən] n. [化学] 氢

Task 3　Overview of New Energy Vehicles

➡ Phrases and Expressions 短语与表达

1. new energy vehicle（NEV）	新能源汽车
2. non-conventional	非常规
3. hybrid electric vehicles（HEV）	混合动力电动汽车
4. wiring harness	线束
5. at the same time	同时
6. battery electric vehicle（BEV）	纯电动汽车
7. fuel cell electric vehicle（FCEV）	燃料电池电动汽车
8. natural gas vehicle	天然气汽车
9. key technology	关键工艺
10. key technique	核心技术

◎ Classroom Activities 课堂活动 ◎

1. Translate the English words in Figure 3-2 into Chinese, and share with classmates. (将图3-2中的英文单词翻译成中文,并与同学们分享。)
2. Engine identification—matching words game(发动机识别——图片与其英文名称匹配识别):选择与显示的发动机图片正确匹配的英文名称。单击OK键,循环学习,直到掌握各种类型发动机的英文表达(游戏操作方法及截屏说明在信息化教学教案里;动态的游戏课件在信息化资源里)。

◎ Grammar Notes 语法注释 ◎

　　The batteries used in the hybrid electric vehicles can recover energy from braking and other conditions.
　　used in the hybrid electric vehicles 是过去分词短语,做 batteries 的后置定语;from braking and other conditions 是介词短语,做 energy 的后置定语。全句可翻译为:混合电动汽车所使用的电池可回收来自制动等工况下的能量。

◎ Text Notes 课文注释 ◎

1. New energy vehicles refer to vehicles that adopt unconventional vehicle fuels as power sources (or use conventional fuels but adopt new vehicle power devices), integrate advanced technologies in vehicle power control and drive, and form advanced technical principles, new technologies and new structures.

新能源汽车是指采用非常规的车用燃料作为动力来源（或使用常规的车用燃料但采用新型车载动力装置），综合车辆的动力控制和驱动方面的先进技术，形成的技术原理先进，具有新技术、新结构的汽车。

2. A hybrid electric vehicle is a hybrid-type electric vehicle powered by more than one energy converter, that is, an electric vehicle using a battery and a secondary energy unit.

混合动力电动汽车是由一种以上的能量转换器提供动力的混合型电动汽车，即使用蓄电池和次级能源的电动汽车。

3. A battery electric vehicle is a vehicle which is powered by the vehicle power supply, and the wheel travel is driven by motor, and which meets the requirements of the road traffic and safety regulations.

纯电动汽车是以车载电源为动力，用电动机驱动车轮行驶，符合道路交通、安全法规各项要求的车辆。

4. The battery electric vehicle has a wide application prospect, and has the advantages with no pollution, low noise and high energy efficiency.

纯电动汽车应用前景广泛，具有无污染、低噪声、高能效等优点。

5. A fuel cell electric vehicle is a new type of vehicle that uses hydrogen and methanol as fuel to generate an electric current through the chemical reactions, and is powered by an electric motor.

燃料电池电动汽车是指以氢气、甲醇等为燃料，通过化学反应产生电流，依靠电动机驱动的新型汽车。

Exercises 练习

Part I Answer the questions according to the text.

1) What is the new energy vehicle?
2) What are the advantages of hybrid electric vehicle?
3) What is the fuel cell electric vehicle?

Part II Translate the following into English.

1) 新能源汽车   2) 传统燃料
3) 天然气汽车   4) 纯电动汽车
5) 燃料电池电动汽车

Part III Translate the following into Chinese.

1) battery module   2) electric motor
3) wiring harness   4) hybrid electric vehicles
5) chemical reaction

Task 3 Overview of New Energy Vehicles

Part IV Translate the following sentences into English.

1) 混合动力电动汽车多采用传统燃料的燃油发动机与电力的混合方式，其关键技术为混合动力系统，它直接影响到整车的性能。
2) 新能源汽车主要包括混合动力电动汽车（HEV）、纯电动汽车（BEV）、燃料电池电动汽车（FCEV）、天然气汽车和其他新能源汽车等。
3) 天然气燃料具有低污染、低成本、安全性能高等优点，但动力性能较低，不便储运。

译文答案

发音训练

Task 4

Vehicle Information Displaying System and Services
汽车信息显示系统及检修

学习目标：
1. 掌握汽车仪表板的组成、作用等的英文术语、词汇；
2. 掌握汽车信息显示屏中用英语标识的术语、词汇；
3. 能读懂汽车信息显示系统相关的英文资料并能进行中英文互译；
4. 能根据汽车信息显示系统维修的英文指示进行维修操作；
5. 能读懂汽车信息显示屏中用英语标识的报警状态。

 Text 课文

Vehicle Information Displaying System and Services

The vehicle information displaying system is one of the important systems of the automobile. The driver can know whether the cars, especially the various operating parameters of the engine are normal or not in order to take timely measures to prevent the occurrence of physical and mechanical accidents.

Traditional instruments widely use the combination analog displaying instruments, and various measuring instruments are fixed on the dashboard in front of the driver's seat. The instrumentations in different vehicle instrument panels are not the same. As is shown in Figure 4-1, it is a typical combination car instrument panel.

The instruments commonly used include speedometer, engine tachometer, oil pressure gauge, water temperature gauge, fuel gauge, ammeter, etc. Changes of the monitored object's status are directly shown in most instruments through the sensors.

With the development of automotive electronic technology, multifunctional, high-precision instruments with intuitive readings, which are shown by electronic digital and image display, have been used in vehicles continuously. Let's know relevant knowledge

Task 4 Vehicle Information Displaying System and Services

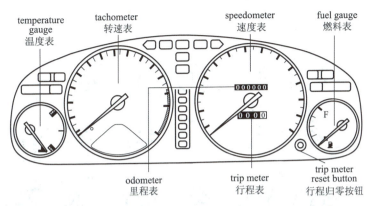

Figure 4 – 1 A typical combination car instrument panel

about the instrument panel of 2019 BMW X5 (Figure 4 – 2).

Figure 4 – 2 The instrument panel of 2019 BMW X5

The 2019 BMW X5's 12.3 in full LCD dashboard is the first time a BMW model has used a liquid crystal instrument with no turbine structure at all. The LCD screen is equipped with iDrive7.0 system, which supports a variety of voice, touch and gesture control methods, and the display content is rich. The central area reserves enough space for the display of the navigation map and is also a multimedia interactive display screen. The black object at the top of the dashboard is the DCS system, which monitors the driver's eyes. when he/she uses the driving assistance system. If the driver's eyes deviate from the front for a long time, the system will remind the driver to concentrate.

These tiny lights in the instrument clusters tracking the operation of the car can provide critical information that could protect you, your passengers and the other drivers on the road.

We've decided to introduce a list of the commonest instrument panels used by different carmakers around the world, although it could be easily expanded to hundreds (Figure 4 – 3).

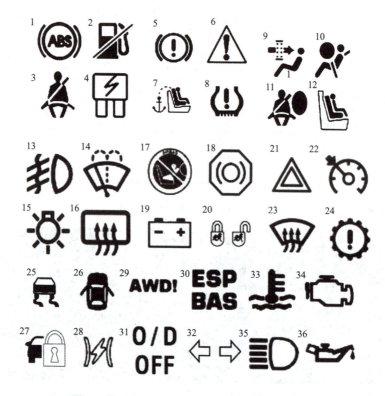

Figure 4 – 3　The commonest instrument panels

1 – ABS warning light; 2 – Low fuel notification; 3 – Seat belt reminder;
4 – Electrical problem warning; 5 – Brake system alert; 6 – Warning light;
7 – Child seat indicator; 8 – Tire pressure monitor; 9 – Air filter;
10 – Front airbag; 11 – Side airbag; 12 – Child seat;
13 – Fog beams indicator; 14 – Windshield wash; 15 – Master lighting switch;
16 – Rear window defrost; 17 – Child seat warning; 18 – Brake fluid malfunction;
19 – Battery warning; 20 – Child safety lock; 21 – Emergency indicator;
22 – Cruise control; 23 – Windshield defrost; 24 – Power train malfunction;
25 – Slip indicator; 26 – Open doors indicator; 27 – Anti-theft system;
28 – Electronic throttle control light; 29 – AWD; 30 – ESP/BAS light;
31 – Overdrive indicator; 32 – Turn signals; 33 – Temperature warning light;
34 – OBD indicator; 35 – High beam light; 36 – Oil pressure warning

Task 4 Vehicle Information Displaying System and Services 23

Toyota Corolla Repair Manual

1. Speedometer

The speedometer shows your speed in kilometers per hour (km/h) and/or miles per hour (mph) depending on type.

Inspect Speedometer

(1) Using a speedometer tester, inspect the speedometer for allowable indication error and check the operation of the odometer.

(2) Check the deflection width of the speed meter indicator: Below 0.5 km/h.

Standard Indication (km/h)	Allowable Range (km/h)
20	21 – 25
40	41.5 – 46
...	...
160	166 – 173

Tire wear and tire over or under inflation will increase the indication error.

Inspect the Output Signal of Vehicle Speed (Figure 4 –4)

While driving the vehicle at the speed of 10 km/h, check the voltage between the terminals C11 –9 and C11 –1 of the combination meter assy. Fluctuation from 10 to 14 V or less is repeated 7 times within 1 sec.

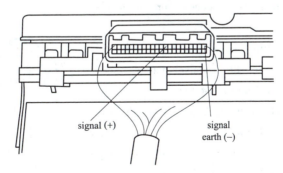

Figure 4 – 4 Inspect the output signal of vehicle speed

Check it with the ignition switch ON and the connector connected.

2. Tachometer

The tachometer shows the engine speed in revolutions per minute (rpm). To protect the engine from damage, never drive with the tachometer needle in the red zone.

Inspect Tachometer

(1) Connect a tune-up test tachometer, and start the engine.

(2) Compare the test with tachometer indications: DC 13.5 V, 25 ℃.

Standard Indication (r/min)   Allowable Range (r/min)

     700   630 – 770

     1,000   900 – 1,100

     …   …

     7,000   6,700 – 7,300

If normal, replace the combination instrument panel; otherwise, repair or replace the wirings and connectors.

3. Fuel Gauge

The fuel gauge displays approximately how much fuel you have in the fuel tank.

Note For proper fuel gauge operation, the ignition switch must be in the OFF position before you add fuel to the fuel tank.

The fuel gauge indicator may vary slightly while the vehicle is in motion. This is the result of fuel movement within the tank. An accurate reading may be obtained with the vehicle on the smooth, level ground.

Inspect the Fuel Gauge (Figure 4 –5)

(1) Disconnect the connector from the sender gauge.

(2) While turning the ignition switch ON, check the position of the receiver gauge needle which should be in "empty" status.

(3) Connect terminals 2 and 3 on the wire harness side connector and turn the ignition switch ON, then check the position of the receiver gauge needle which should be in "full" status.

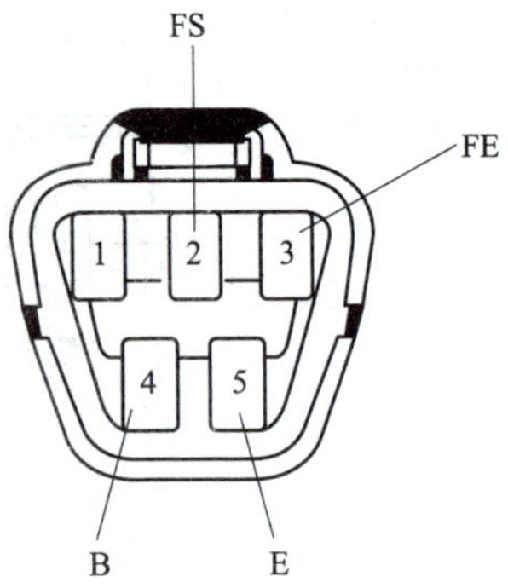

Figure 4 –5 Inspect the fuel gauge

Inspect Fuel Level Warning

(1) Disconnect the connector from the sender gauge.

(2) Turn the ignition switch ON. Check the fuel level needle indicates EMPTY and fuel level warning lights light on.

Task 4 Vehicle Information Displaying System and Services

4. Temperature Gauge

This shows the temperature of the engine's coolant. During normal operation, the pointer should rise from the bottom blue mark to about the middle of the gauge. In severe driving conditions, such as very hot weather or a long period of uphill driving the pointer may rise to the upper white mark. If it reaches the red (Hot) mark, the engine is overheated and may be damaged.

If your engine overheats:

(1) Pull off the road as soon as it is safely possible.

(2) Turn off the engine.

(3) Let the engine cool.

(4) Check the coolant level following the instructions on checking and adding coolant to your engine, and see the Engine Coolant in the Index.

Inspect the Water Temperature Receiver Gauge Warning Light

(1) Disconnect the connector from the sender gauge.

(2) Turn the ignition switch ON, and check the position of the water temperature receiver gauge needle which should indicate "cool."

(3) While ground terminal 2 is on the wire harness side, check the water temperature receiver gauge needle which should indicate "hot."

New Words 生词

1. various [ˈvɛəriəs] adj. 不同的，各种各样的，多方面的
2. parameter [pəˈræmitə] n. 参数，参量
3. occurrence [əˈkʌrəns] n. 发生
4. speedometer [spiˈdɔmitə] n. 速度表
5. tachometer [tæˈkɔmitə] n. 转速表
6. ammeter [ˈæmitə] n. 电流表
7. intuitive [inˈtju(:)itiv] adj. 直觉的
8. continuously [kənˈtinjuəsli] adv. 不断地，连续地
9. deflection [diˈflekʃən] n. 偏斜，偏转，偏差
10. fluctuation [ˌflʌktjuˈeiʃən] n. 波动，起伏
11. needle [ˈniːdl] n. 指针
12. accurate [ˈækjurit] adj. 正确的，精确的

➡ Phrases and Expressions 短语与表达

1. combination car instrument panel　　汽车组合仪表板
2. oil pressure gauge　　机油压力表
3. water temperature gauge　　水温表
4. fuel gauge　　燃油表
5. tune-up　　调整
6. fuel tank　　燃油箱
7. wire harness　　线束

● Classroom Activities 课堂活动

1. Translate the English words in Figure 4-1 into Chinese, and share with classmates. (将图4-1中的英文单词翻译成中文,并与同学们分享。)

2. Flashcard identification: Let the students try to match the English flashcards with the Chinese ones. (卡片识别:让同学们尝试英文卡片与中文卡片的匹配活动。活动方法:以小组为学习单位,小组成员之间进行中、英文卡片的匹配;选出两组代表进行比赛。)

   Flashcards(卡片):display 显示, inspect 检查, check 检查, turn on 打开, repair 维修, connect 连接, disconnect 断开, meter 量表, needle 指针, warning light 警示灯, speedometer 速度表, vehicle 车辆, gauge 量表, odometer 里程表, dashboard 仪表板, panel 仪表板, tachometer 转速表, pressure 压力, fuel 燃油, oil 机油。

3. Smart-board words game. 电子白板游戏法:应用交互式电子白板互动课堂工具,设计单词学习游戏,让学生进行单词游戏训练。

   Scrambled words quiz game(单词重组游戏):在训练模板上输入5个单词,通过移动字母小球的顺序而获得正确单词的游戏方式(计时)来完成这一组单词的重组训练(游戏操作方法及截屏说明放在信息化教学教案里;动态的游戏课件与教案一起均放在信息化教学资源文件夹里)。

● Text Notes 课文注释

1. The driver can know whether the cars, especially the various operating parameters of the engine are normal or not in order to take timely measures to prevent the occurrence of physical and mechanical accidents.

   驾驶员能随时了解汽车的状况,特别是发动机的各种工作参数是否正常,以便及时采取措施,防止发生人身和机械事故。

Task 4 Vehicle Information Displaying System and Services

2. Traditional instruments widely use the combination analog displaying instruments, and various measuring instruments are fixed on the dashboard in front of the driver's seat.
   传统仪表广泛使用组合式模拟显示仪表,各种测量仪表集中在驾驶员座位前方的仪表板上。

3. The instruments commonly used include speedometer, engine tachometer, oil pressure gauge, water temperature gauge, fuel gauge, ammeter, etc.
   常用的仪表有车速里程表、发动机转速表、机油压力表、水温表、燃油表、电流表等。

4. Changes of the monitored object's status are directly shown in most instruments through the sensors.
   被监测对象的状态变化通过各种传感器获得,在大部分仪表中直接显示出来。

5. Using a speedometer tester, inspect the speedometer for allowable indication error and check the operation of the odometer.
   用车速表测试仪检查车速表的允许指示误差,并检查里程表的工作情况。

6. While driving the vehicle at the speed of 10 km/h, check the voltage between the terminals C11 – 9 and C11 – 1 of the combination meter assy.
   以 10 km/h 的车速驾驶车辆,检测组合仪表总成端子 C11 – 9 与 C11 – 1 之间的电压。

7. During normal operation, the pointer should rise from the bottom blue mark to about the middle of the gauge.
   正常驾驶时,表的长针应从表的下端蓝色标记指到大约中间的位置。

Safety Tips 安全提示

用电安全:
(1) 操作电力工具时,应使用接地正确的三相插孔和加长导线,而对于某些工具,则仅使用两相插头。
(2) 对切断或受损电线进行维修或更换时,应确保它们双层绝缘,以免触电。
(3) 不使用时,勿将电线放置在地上,以免将人绊倒。
(4) 若电线位于人流量大的地方,则应把它用带子扎起来进行保护。

Exercises 练习

Part I Choose the best answers from the following choices according to the text.

1. The _____ tells you how many miles (kilometers) per hour your vehicle is

moving.

    A. odometer   B. trip meter   C. speedometer   D. tachometer

2. The _____ tells you the total number of miles (kilometers) your vehicle has been driven.

    A. odometer   B. trip meter   C. speedometer   D. tachometer

3. The _____ tells you how many miles (kilometers) your car has been driven since the last reset.

    A. odometer   B. trip meter   C. speedometer   D. tachometer

4. The _____ shows you the engine speed in revolutions per minute (rpm).

    A. odometer   B. trip meter   C. speedometer   D. tachometer

5. To protect the engine from damage, never drive with the tachometer needle in the _____.

    A. white mark   B. red zone   C. blue mark   D. yellow zone

6. The _____ displays how much fuel you have in the fuel tank.

    A. oil pressure gauge   B. fuel gauge

    C. water temperature gauge   D. ammeter

7. The temperature gauge shows the temperature of the engine's _____.

    A. oil   B. coolant   C. incoming air   D. exhaust

Part Ⅱ　Translate the following into English.

1. 线束　　　　　　　　　　2. 组合仪表总成

3. 连接器　　　　　　　　　4. 燃油液位警告灯

5. 平地　　　　　　　　　　6. 燃油表

7. 接线柱(端子)　　　　　　8. 负极导线

Part Ⅲ　Translate the following into Chinese.

1. instrument panel　　　　　2. disconnect

3. ground　　　　　　　　　4. on-board computer

5. shut off　　　　　　　　　6. warning light

7. tail light switch　　　　　　8. overheat

Part Ⅳ　Translate the following sentences into Chinese.

1. Using a speedometer tester, inspect the speedometer for allowable indication error and check the operation of the odometer.

2. Check the deflection width of the speed meter indicator.

3. Tire wear and tire over or under inflation will increase the indication error.

Task 4 Vehicle Information Displaying System and Services

4. While ground terminal 2 is on the wire harness side, check the water temperature receiver gauge needle which should indicate "hot."

Part V Complete the question based on the graphs below.

Now, most of the freshmen often can not read a variety of indicator lights on the instrument panel. There are some indicator lights as follows. Please depict their purposes respectively.

Task 5

EFI System Operating Principle and DTC Identification
电子燃油喷射系统工作原理及故障诊断代码识别

学习目标：
1. 掌握电控燃油喷射系统的英文专业术语；
2. 熟悉故障代码的识别及检查方法。

 Text 课文

5.1 Electronic Fuel Injection System Operation

EFI (Electronic Fuel Injection) engine is a new type of internal combustion engine, through the microcomputer. It can control the electronic fuel injectors to inject fuel to the cylinders of the engine according to the engine's load. It makes the digital ignition and fuel injection function into realization: reducing fuel consumption, emissions improvement. At the same time, it is easy to start and break out at any moment with the stable idle speed (Figure 5 – 1).

EFI System Classification

There are different types of gasoline injection systems used in automobiles. The three basic arrangements in EFI systems are the single-point fuel injection, multi-point fuel injection (Figure 5 – 2) and gasoline direct injection (Figure 5 – 3, Figure 5 – 4).

- **Single-point fuel injection**

In a Single-point fuel injection (also called TBI, throttle body fuel injection), fuel is injected into the area around the throttle valve, where air velocity is at a maximum, thus ensuring fuel droplets are thoroughly atomized and will be distributed throughout the air mass.

Task 5 EFI System Operating Principle and DTC Identification

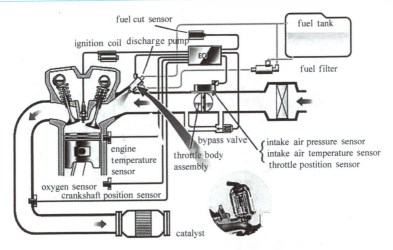

Figure 5 – 1   Electronic fuel injection system

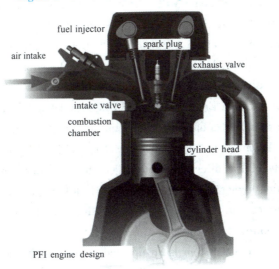

Figure 5 – 2   Multi-point fuel injection system

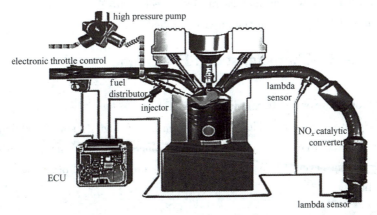

Figure 5 – 3   Gasoline direct injection system

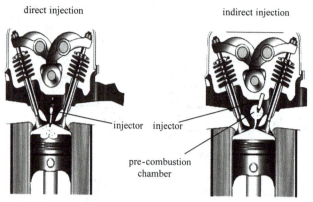

Figure 5-4　Differences in operation with direct injection and indirect injection

- **Multi-point fuel injection**

Multi-point fuel injection (MPI, also called PFI, port fuel injection) injects fuel into the intake ports just upstream of each cylinder's intake valve, rather than at a central point within an intake manifold. MPI systems can be sequential, in which injection is timed to coincide with each cylinder's intake stroke.

- **Gasoline direct injection**

In a Direct Injection Engine (Gasoline Direct Injection, GDI), fuel is injected into the combustion chamber as opposed to injection before the intake valve (petrol engine) or a separate pre-combustion chamber (diesel engine). By virtue of better dispersion and homogeneity of the directly injected fuel, the cylinders and pistons are cooled, thereby permitting higher compression ratios and earlier ignition timing, with resultant enhanced power output. More precise management of the fuel injection event also enables better control of emissions.

The direct injection system is an updated version of the multi-point fuel injection system. The difference between the direct injection system and the multi-point fuel injection system is that the fuel is injected directly into the combustion chamber at the most appropriate time by the computer-controlled injector.

5.2　Characteristic of EFI Engine

1. Good Power Performance of EFI Engine

The fuel injection precision of EFI system is very high, a simple catalytic can meets national V's required. So, the exhaust resistance is small, output power of engine accordingly big, even it is used for a long time, the possibility of exhaust pipe block up is very little.

Task 5　EFI System Operating Principle and DTC Identification

2. Good Start

The EFI system has two temperature sensors, can apperceive what the environment temperature is and whether the engine is in hot or cold status. According to the information, the computer unit ECU can calculate the optimal oil volume, and make it break out at any moment, no need to wait for the warming up of the motorcycle.

3. Simple System and Convenient to Maintenance

The EFI system is simple and easy to understand, and convenient to maintenance. Any kind of electronic control gasoline injection device is composed of three parts: oil injection circuit, sensor group and electronic control unit.

4. Engine's Overheat Protect

When continually at idle speed, because of lack of cooling air, the engine can be overheat easily and the fuel tank will lose fuel because the fuel tank is baked. So, when the engine's temperature is over certain limit, the EFI system can force and stop the running of the engine.

5.3　Diagnostic Trouble Code Identification Cases

Case 1. DTC: P0100 — Mass Air Flow Sensor Circuit Malfunction

Trouble Areas:

(1) Open or short in the air flow meter circuit.

(2) The air flow meter.

(3) The ECM.

Case 2. DTC: P0110 — Intake Air Temperature Sensor Circuit Malfunction

Trouble Areas:

(1) Open or short in the intake air temperature sensor circuit.

(2) The intake air temperature sensor (inside air flow meter).

(3) The ECM.

Case 3. DTC: P0120 — Throttle Position Sensor Circuit Malfunction

Trouble Areas:

(1) Open or short in the throttle position sensor circuit.

(2) The throttle position sensor.

(3) The ECM.

Case 4. DTC: P0505 — Idle Control System Malfunction

Trouble Areas:

(1) Open or short in ISC valve circuit.

(2) The ISC valve is stuck or closed.

(3) Open or short in the A/C switch circuit.

(4) The air induction system.

(5) The ECM.

Circuit Malfunction Inspection Procedure of DTC P0505

(1) Perform active tests by the handheld tester (Check the operation of the ISC valve).

    a. Warm up the engine to the normal operating temperature.

    b. Switch off all the accessories.

    c. Switch off the A/C.

    d. Shift the lever into the neutral position.

    e. Connect the handheld tester to the DLC3 on the vehicle.

    f. Check the difference of the engine speeds in less than 5 seconds and more than 5 seconds (Difference of engine speeds: more than 100 rpm).

    Yes — Check for intermittent problems.

    No — (2).

(2) Check the harness and connector.

    a. Disconnect the ISC valve connector.

    b. Turn the ignition switch on.

    c. Measure the voltage between terminals +B and E01 of the ISC valve connector (9 – 14 V).

    Yes — Repair or replace the harness and connector.

    No — (3).

(3) Check the harness and connector.

    a. Disconnect the ECM E19 connector.

    b. Disconnect the ISC valve connector.

    c. Check the continuity between terminals RSO of the ECM connector and RSO of the ISC valve connector (Resistance: 1 Ω or less).

    d. Check for short between terminals RSO of the ECM connector and E01 of the ISC valve connector (Resistance: 1 MΩ or more).

    No — Repair or replace the harness and connector.

Task 5 EFI System Operating Principle and DTC Identification

   Yes — (4).
(4) Inspect the throttle body idle speed control valve assembly.
   No — Replace the throttle body idle speed control valve assembly.
   Yes — Check and replace the ECM.

New Words 生词

1. consumption [kənˈsʌmpʃn] n. 消费；消耗
2. emission [ɪˈmɪʃn] n.（光、热等的）发射，散发；喷射
3. injector [ɪnˈdʒektə] n. 喷油器；注射器
4. throttle [ˈθrɒtl] n. 节流阀；[车辆]风门；喉咙
5. droplet [ˈdrɒplət] n. 小滴，微滴
6. atomize [ˈætəmaɪz] n. 将……喷成雾状
7. upstream [ˌʌpˈstriːm] adv. 向（在）上游；逆流地
8. cylinder [ˈsɪlɪndə(r)] n. 圆筒；气缸
9. sequential [sɪˈkwenʃl] adj. 连续的；有顺序的；
10. homogeneity [ˌhoʊməudʒəˈniːəti] n. 同质；同种；同次性
11. piston [ˈpɪstən] n. 活塞
12. appropriate [əˈprəupriət] adj. 适当的；恰当的；合适的
13. overheat [ˌəuvəˈhiːt] vi. 过热
14. accessory [əkˈseəri] n. 配件；附件
15. connector [kəˈnektə(r)] n. 连接器，连接头
16. open [ˈəupən] adj. 断路的
17. short [ʃɔːt] adj. 短路的
18. diagnostic [ˌdaɪəɡˈnɒstɪk] adj. 诊断的
19. identification [aɪˌdentɪfɪˈkeɪʃn] n. 鉴定，识别
20. malfunction [ˌmælˈfʌŋkʃn] n. 故障，失灵

➡ Phrases and Expressions 短语与表达

1. ISC valve   怠速控制阀
2. +B (battery)   蓄电池
3. DLC3   诊断传输接头3
4. E01 (computer ground)   计算机搭铁线
5. gasoline direct injection   汽油机缸内直喷系统
6. temperature sensor   温度传感器
7. electronic fuel injection (EFI) 电子控制燃油喷射
8. throttle position sensor   节气门位置传感器
9. hand-held tester   手持式测试仪
10. inspection procedure   检查步骤

11. multi-point fuel injection(MPI)   多点燃油喷射
12. needle valve   针阀
13. port fuel injection   进气口燃油喷射
14. RSO(rotor solenoid)   转子电磁线圈
15. single-point fuel injection(SPI)   单点燃油喷射
16. throttle body injection   节气门体燃油喷射
17. throttle valve   节气门
18. trouble area   故障可能发生部位
19. VC(Air flow Meter)   空气流量计

Classroom Activities 课堂活动

1. Translate the English words in Figure 5-1 ~ Figure 5-3 into Chinese; share these words with your classmates. (将图 5-1 ~ 图 5-3 中的英文单词翻译成中文;并与同学们分享。)

2. Smart-board spelling words game 电子白板拼词游戏法:应用交互式电子白板 Smart-board 互动课堂工具,设计单词学习游戏,让学生进行单词拼写训练。
在训练模板上输入10个单词(单词可替换,游戏可复制),在拼词训练的游戏画面中,可选择 Soccer 或 Basketball 或 Tomato splat 的游戏表现形式来提取字母进行拼词训练。学生可在老师及同伴的协助下参与训练,以增强课堂中的师生互动、生生互动(游戏操作方法及截屏说明,详见信息化教学教案;动态的游戏课件与教案均放在信息化教学资源文件夹里)。

Grammar Notes 语法注释

Fuel is injected into the area around the throttle valve.
燃油被喷射到节气门周围的区域。
在专业英语中,常需要运用被动语句表达某个机构动作以后产生的结果,侧重于结果,英语多用 is / am / are + 及物动词的过去分词来传达命令。

Text Notes 课文注释

1. It makes the digital ignition and fuel injection function come into realization: reducing fuel consumption, emissions improvement. 它使数字点火和喷油功能得以实现:降低油耗,改善排放。

Task 5 EFI System Operating Principle and DTC Identification

2. Fuel is injected into the area around the throttle valve, where air velocity is at a maximum. 燃油被喷进空气速度达到最大值的节气门周围区域。

3. MPI systems can be sequential, in which injection is timed to coincide with each cylinder's intake stroke. MPI 系统可以是连续的,其中喷射时间与每个气缸的进气冲程相一致。

4. The EFI system has two temperature sensors, can apperceive what the environment temperature is and whether the engine is in hot or cold status. EFI 系统有两个温度传感器,可以感知环境温度和发动机的冷热状态。

5. Open or short in air flow meter circuit.
   空气流量计电路断路或短路。

6. Connect the handheld tester to the DLC3 on the vehicle.
   将手持式测试仪连接到车辆上的诊断传输接头 3。

7. Check the continuity between terminals RSO of the ECM connector and RSO of the ISC valve connector (Resistance: 1 Ω or less).
   检查在 ECM 连接器和 ISC 阀连接器的转子电磁线圈接线柱之间的通路(电阻值应为 1 Ω 或更少)。

Safety Tips 安全提示

(1) 对燃油系统部件进行检修前,要先泄放燃油系统的压力。

(2) 安全使用空气软管:空气喷嘴使用不当会使人失明或失聪,通往空气喷嘴的压缩空气压力必须降至 206 kPa 以下。如果用空气喷嘴吹干或清洁零件,则勿将气流对准周围的人。空气软管不使用时应卷起来并妥善放置。

Exercises 练习

Part I Choose the best answers from the following choices according to the text.

1. There are different types of _____ injection systems used in automobiles.
   A. throttle valve   B. ISC valve   C. gasoline   D. ECU

2. Single-point fuel injection also called _____.
   A. TBI   B. PFI   C. EFI   D. GDI

3. MPI systems can be sequential, in which injection is timed to coincide with each cylinder's _____.
   A. air mass   B. intake stroke   C. intake valve   D. throttle body

4. More precise management of the fuel injection event also enables better control of _____.

A. port   B. throttle valve shaft
C. valve   D. emissions

5. The EFI system has two temperature sensors, can apperceive what the environment temperature is and whether the _____ is in hot or cold status.

A. engine   B. stick   C. rickety   D. move

6. When the engine's temperature is over certain limit, the EFI system can _____ and stop the running of engine.

A. force   B. fuel   C. fluid   D. oil

Part II   Translate the following into English.

1. 空气流量计   2. 节气门
3. 短路   4. 怠速控制阀
5. 断路   6. 电路故障
7. 位置传感器   8. 连接器

Part III   Translate the following into Chinese.

1. warm up   2. intermittent problem
3. resistance value   4. identification
5. switch off   6. accessory
7. trouble code   8. malfunction

Part IV   Translate the following sentences into Chinese.

1. The three basic arrangements in EFI systems are the single-point fuel injection, multi-point fuel injection and gasoline direct injection.

2. The EFI system is simple and easy to understand, and convenient to maintenance.

3. So, when the engine's temperature is over certain limit, the EFI system can force and stop the running of engine.

4. Measure the voltage between terminals + B and E01 of the ISC valve connector (9 - 14 V).

5. Check for short between terminals RSO of the ECM connector and E01 of the ISC valve connector (Resistance: 1 MΩ or more).

Part V   Read the following passage and then answer the following questions.

The air flow meter uses a platinum hot wire. The hot wire air flow meter consists of a platinum hot wire, a temperature sensor and a control circuit installed in a plastic housing. The hot wire air flow meter works on the principle that the hot wire and the

Task 5 EFI System Operating Principle and DTC Identification

temperature sensor located in the intake air bypass of the housing detect any changes in the intake air temperature.

The hot wire is maintained at the set temperature by controlling the current flow through the hot wire. This current flow is then measured as the output voltage of the air flow meter.

The circuit is constructed so that the platinum hot wire and temperature sensor provide a bridge circuit, with the power transistor controlled so that the potential of A and B remains equal to maintain the set temperature.

1. How many parts does the hot wire air flow meter consist of?
    A. One.　　　　B. Two.　　　　C. Three.　　　　D. Four.
2. What is installed in the plastic housing?
    A. A control circuit.
    B. A platinum hot wire.
    C. A platinum hot wire and a temperature sensor.
    D. A platinum hot wire, a temperature sensor and a control circuit.
3. What is located in the intake air bypass of the housing?
    A. The temperature sensor.　　　　B. The hot wire and the temperature sensor.
    C. The hot wire.　　　　　　　　　D. The intake air bypass.
4. How is the hot wire maintained at the set temperature?
    A. By controlling hot wire.
    B. By controlling the current flow.
    C. By controlling the current flow through the hot wire.
    D. By controlling the temperature.

译文答案

发音训练

Task 6

Cooling System Service Manual
冷却系统维修手册

学习目标：

1. 掌握冷却系统的专业英文词汇；
2. 熟悉汽车专业英语的表达习惯；
3. 能理解冷却系统的英文维修手册。

 Text 课文

Cooling System Operation

The cooling system controls temperature by heat transfer. Heat always moves from a hot object to a cooler object, so the cooling system transfers heat from the engine cylinder to the circulating coolant. Then the coolant transfers heat to the airflow through the radiator. The temperature control and heat transfer are based on the pressure of the system and coolant circulation (Figure 6–1).

The pressures at the water pump outlet and in the water jackets near the combustion chambers are highest. The system pressure at the water pump inlet is lowest. The pressure is generated by the water pump and controlled by variable restrictions, like the thermostat, the heater control valve and valves in the radiator cap. The system also has fixed restrictions, such as orifices in the water jackets and passages in the radiator.

Cooling System Repair Manual

Before servicing the cooling system, you need to pay particular attention to the following:

Task 6 Cooling System Service Manual

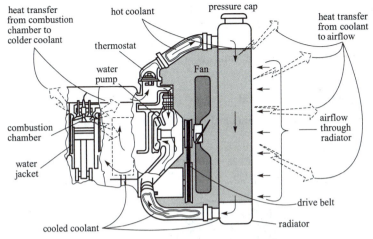

Figure 6 – 1 Cooling system operation

To avoid the danger of being burned, do not remove the reservoir cap while the engine and the radiator are still hot, as fluid and steam can be blown out under pressure.

1. Inspect the Cooling System for Leaks
(1) Fill the radiator with coolant and attach a radiator cap tester.
(2) Warm up the engine.
(3) Pump the radiator cap tester to 118 kPa, and check the pressure does not drop.

Hint If the pressure drops, check the hoses, radiator or water pump for leaks. If no external leaks are found, check the heater core, the cylinder block and the head.

2. Check Engine Coolant Level at Reservoir
The engine coolant level should be between the "LOW" and "FULL" line.

Notice The engine coolant level is checked when the engine is cold only.

Hint If low, check for leaks and add coolant up to the "FULL" line.

3. Check Engine Coolant Quality
(1) Remove the radiator cap (Please pay particular attention to be burned).
(2) Check if there are any excessive deposits of rust or scale around the radiator cap and radiator filler holes. The coolant should be free from oil.

Hint If excessively dirty, replace the coolant.

(3) Reinstall the radiator cap.

4. Inspect the Thermostat

There are three ways to check the thermostat, one of which is "Heat the Water."

Hint The thermostat is numbered with the valve opening temperature, as is shown in Figure 6-2.

Figure 6-2 The thermostat numbered with the valve opening temperature

(1) Remove the thermostat from the engine and put it close.

(2) Immerse the thermostat in water and gradually heat the water (Figure 6-3).

(3) Check the valve opening temperature (80 ℃ - 84 ℃).

Hint If the valve opening temperature is not as specified, replace the thermostat.

(4) Check the valve lift (10 mm or more at 90 ℃) (Figure 6-4).

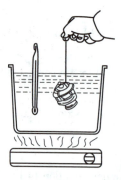

Figure 6-3 The thermostat immersed in water and the water heated gradually

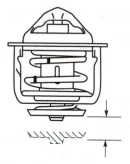

Figure 6-4 The valve lift being checked

Task 6　Cooling System Service Manual 43

Hint　If the valve lift is not as specified, replace the thermostat.

(5) Check that the valve is fully closed when the thermostat is at low temperatures (below 77 ℃).

Hint　If the valve is not closed, replace the thermostat.

5. Coolant Replacement

A coolant change should be performed at every two years or 36,000 km.

(1) Drain coolant (when the engine is cold).
a. Remove the radiator cap.
b. Loosen the radiator drain plug and drain the coolant.

(2) Add coolant (always check the owner's manual for the specifications for the recommended engine coolant).
a. Tighten the radiator drain plug, and pour coolant into the radiator until it overflows.

Hint　Press hard the radiator inlet and outlet hoses several times. If the coolant level gets lower, pour coolant.

b. Tighten the radiator cap.
c. Pour engine coolant into the reservoir tank until it reaches full line.
d. Warm up the engine until the thermostat valve begins to open.

Hint　Press hard the radiator inlet and outlet hoses several times during the warming up.

e. Stop the engine and wait until the coolant temperature gets cold. Then remove the radiator cap to check the coolant level.
f. If the level gets lower, perform the procedures above again.
g. If the level does not get lower, adjust the reservoir tank coolant level.

(3) Inspect engine coolant leak.
a. Fill the radiator with coolant and attach a radiator cap tester.
b. Pump it to 118 kPa and check leakage.

New Words 生词

1. coolant [ˈkuːlənt] n. 冷却剂,冷却液
2. radiator [ˈreidieitə] n. 散热器,水箱
3. thermostat [ˈθəːməstæt] n. 节温器
4. generate [ˈdʒenəˌreit] v. 产生,发生
5. leak [liːk] n. 泄漏
6. inspect [inˈspekt] v. 检查
7. reservoir [ˈrezəvwaː] n. 储液罐
8. quality [ˈkwɔliti] n. 品质
9. excessive [ikˈsesiv] adj. 过多的
10. replace [ri(ː)ˈpleis] v. 取代,更换
11. deposit [diˈpɔzit] n. 沉积物
12. rust [rʌst] n. 锈 v. 生锈
13. scale [skeil] n. 水垢
14. hint [hint] n. 暗示,提示
15. orifice [ˈɔrifis] n. 孔,口
16. immerse [iˈməːs] v. 沉浸于,使陷入
17. rinse [rins] v. 冲洗

Phrases and Expressions 短语与表达

1. water pump —— 水泵
2. water jacket —— 水套
3. combustion chamber —— 燃烧室
4. variable restriction —— 可变约束
5. blow out —— 喷出
6. radiator cap tester —— 散热器加水口盖测试仪
7. heater core —— 暖风机芯
8. cylinder block —— 气缸体
9. cylinder head —— 气缸盖
10. Heat the Water —— 热水法
11. free from —— 被免除的
12. relief valve —— 减压阀
13. radiator drain plug —— 散热器放液塞

Classroom Activities 课堂活动

1. Flashcard identification: Let the students try to match the English flashcards with the Chinese ones. (卡片识别:让同学们尝试英文卡片与中文卡片的匹配活动。活动方法:以小组为学习单位,小组成员之间进行中、英文卡片的匹配活动;选出两组代表进行比赛。)

   Flashcards(卡片): inspect 检查, check 检查, replace 更换, remove 拆下, drain 排

Task 6 Cooling System Service Manual

放,coolant 冷却液,thermostat 节温器,radiator 散热器,water pump 水泵,water jacket 水套。

2. Translate the English words in Figure 6 – 1 into Chinese, and share with classmates. (将图 6 – 1 中的英文单词翻译成中文,并与同学们分享。)
3. Smart-board words game. 电子白板游戏法:应用交互式电子白板互动课堂工具, 设计学习游戏,让学生在游戏中训练单词。
   (1)Scrambled words quiz game.(单词重组游戏。)
   (2)Image-matching activity.(图片与英文词汇匹配活动。)
   (游戏操作方法及截屏说明在信息化教学教案里;动态的游戏课件在信息化教学 资源文件夹里。)

Grammar Notes 语法注释

The pressure is generated by the water pump and controlled by variable restrictions. 句中的 be generated by 由……产生、be controlled by 由……控制,均为被动语态, generated 和 controlled 是过去分词。若将 The pressure is generated by the water pump 变为主动语态,by 后面的部分则为主语:The water pump generates pressure. 全句译为:(冷却系统的)压力由水泵产生,并受各种可变约束的控制。

Text Notes 课文注释

1. The pressures at the water pump outlet and in the water jackets near the combustion chambers are highest
   冷却系统的压力在水泵出口和燃烧室附近的水套里的压力是最高的。
2. Fill the radiator with coolant and attach a radiator cap tester.
   往散热器中加注冷却液,装上散热器加水口盖测试仪。
3. Check if there are any excessive deposits of rust or scale around the radiator cap and radiator filler holes. The coolant should be free from oil.
   检查散热器加水口盖和加水口周围是否有较多的锈和水垢的沉积,冷却液中应 没有机油。
4. The thermostat is numbered with the valve opening temperature.
   节温器上标有阀的开启温度。
5. Remove the thermostat from the engine and put it close.
   将节温器从发动机上拆下来,并使它处于关闭状态。
6. Check the valve lift.
   检查阀门升程。
7. Loosen the radiator drain plug and drain the coolant.
   松开散热器放液塞并放出冷却液。
8. Stop the engine and wait until the coolant temperature gets cold. Then remove the

radiator cap to check the coolant level.

使发动机停机,等到冷却液变凉。然后拆下散热器加水口盖以便检查冷却液液位。

Safety Tips 安全提示

冷却液是防冻剂和水的混合物。虽然误食用没使用的防冻剂会导致死亡,但它不属于危险物资。废旧的防冻剂可能具有危险性,这是由发动机和其他冷却系统中零部件的金属(包括铁、铝、铜、钢和来自老式散热器及水箱中的铅等)溶解在防冻剂中造成的。

处理废旧冷却液的几点建议:

(1) 冷却剂应当场回收或送至别处回收。

(2) 废旧冷却剂应储存在密封容器里,并贴上标签。

(3) 在取得相关管理部门许可的情况下,废旧冷却剂可被倒入城市下水道。

Exercises 练习

Part I Choose the best answers from the following choices according to the text.

1. The cooling system controls temperature by _____.
    A. heat transfer   B. airflow   C. sensors   D. ECU

2. The cooling system transfers heat from the engine cylinder to the _____.
    A. coolant   B. circulating coolant
    C. circulation   D. coolant circulation

3. The temperature control and heat transfer are based _____ the system pressure and the coolant circulation.
    A. in   B. to   C. on   D. by

4. To avoid the danger of _____, do not remove the reservoir cap while the engine and radiator are still hot.
    A. be burned   B. burned
    C. burn   D. being burned

5. Fill the radiator _____ coolant and attach a radiator cap tester.
    A. with   B. use   C. in   D. on

6. If no external leaks _____, check the heater core, the cylinder block and the head.
    A. find   B. are found   C. found   D. be found

7. The engine coolant level is checked when the engine is _____ only.
    A. hot   B. warm   C. cold   D. cool

Task 6 Cooling System Service Manual

8. Check that the valve is fully closed when the thermostat is at low temperatures (below 77 ℃). If it is not closed, replace the _____.
   A. radiator B. water jacket
   C. coolant D. thermostat
9. Using a radiator cap tester, slowly pump the tester and check that air is coming from the vacuum valve. If air is not coming from the _____, replace the reservoir cap.
   A. vacuum valve B. pump C. tester D. radiator
10. Add coolant (Always check the owner's manual for the _____ for the recommended engine coolant).
    A. special B. specifications C. specification D. specified

Part II Translate the following into English.
1. 散热器盖   2. 冷却液品质
3. 软管   4. 暖风机芯
5. 气缸盖   6. 阀门升程
7. 更换节温器   8. 减压阀
9. 开启压力   10. 测试仪最大读数
11. 散热器排液塞   12. 规格

Part III Translate the following into Chinese.
1. water pump   2. water jacket
3. deposit   4. thermostat
5. orifice   6. cylinder block
7. tighten   8. loosen
9. pour   10. coolant leak
11. outlet hose   12. combustion chamber

Part IV Translate the following sentences into Chinese.
1. The pressure is generated by the water pump and controlled by variable restrictions, like the thermostat, the heater control valve and valves in the radiator cap.
2. The system also has fixed restrictions, such as orifices in the water jackets and passages in the radiator.
3. Before servicing the cooling system, you need to pay particular attention to the following.
4. Immerse the thermostat in water and gradually heat the water. Check the valve opening temperature (80 ℃ – 84 ℃). If the valve opening temperature is not as

specified, replace the thermostat.

5. A coolant change should be performed at every two years or 36,000 km.

Part V Complete the following questions based on the graphs below.

1. What is the technician holding and checking(Figure 6 – 5)?

2. What part is immersed in water(Figure 6 – 6)? What is the technician doing?

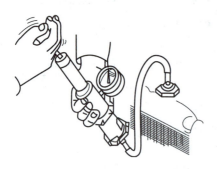

Figure 6 – 5 Part V No. 1

Figure 6 – 6 Part V No. 2

Part VI Read the following passage, then complete the following questions.

Circulation Check

Cooling system service begins with an inspection of all components for damage and leakage. And don't overlook the water pump drive belt. The water pump creates pressure that causes coolant to circulate. Unwanted restrictions in the radiator, the engine or hoses can block circulation, however. The basic way to check circulation is to look for cooler spots in the system.

Run the engine until it's fully warm and the thermostat is open. Then shut off the engine and run your hand over the radiator core from inlet tank to outlet tank to feel for cool spots. Do the same with all the hoses. The radiator and the hoses should be uniformly warm. Any spots cooler than others indicate restrictions, or blockage, in the system.

Are the following statements True or False?

1. Cooling system service begins with an inspection of the water pump drive belt. (   )

2. Cooling system pressure is generated by the water pump. (   )

3. Unwanted restrictions in the system will reduce circulation efficiency. (   )

4. The basic way to check circulation is to look for cooler spots in the system. (   )

5. Run your hand over the radiator core to feel for cool spots when the engine is cold. (   )

Task 6 Cooling System Service Manual   49

6. Run the engine until it's fully warm and the thermostat is open. Then shut off the engine and run your hand over the radiator core and radiator inlet and outlet hoses to feel for cool spots. (   )

7. Any spots cooler than others show that there are restrictions or stoppages in the cooling system. (   )

译文答案

发音训练

Task 7

Ignition System Service Manual
点火系统维修手册

学习目标:

1. 掌握发动机点火系统的组成、作用等的英文术语、词汇;
2. 能读懂发动机点火系统相关的英文资料,并能进行中英文互译;
3. 能根据发动机点火系统维修的英文指示,进行维修操作;
4. 能针对发动机点火系统实物用英文指出各组成部件。

 Text 课文

 Engine Ignition System

The function of an ignition system in the gasoline engine is to transform the voltage from the battery to high-tension voltage, and timely introduce the electricity into the engine cylinder in accordance with the work order of the engine cylinder to ignite the air-fuel mixture by spark, so that the engine can be started normally. The conventional ignition system consists of the battery, the ignition coil, the distributor, the condenser, the ignition switch, the spark plugs, the resistor and the necessary low and high tension wiring.

The ignition coil (Figure 7 - 1) is a simple device—essentially a high-voltage transformer made up of two coils of wire. One coil of wire is called the primary coil. Wrapped around it is the secondary coil. The secondary coil normally has hundreds of times more turns of wire than the primary coil. Current flows from the battery through the primary winding of the coil. The primary coil's current can be suddenly disrupted by the breaker points, or by a solid-state device in an electronic ignition.

If you think the coil looks like an electromagnet, you're right— but it is also an inductor. The key to the coil's operation is what happens when the circuit is suddenly

Task 7 Ignition System Service Manual   51

broken by the points. The magnetic field of the primary coil collapses rapidly. The secondary coil is engulfed by a powerful and changing magnetic field. This field induces a current in the coils—a very high-voltage current (up to 100,000 volts) because of the number of coils in the secondary winding. The secondary coil feeds this voltage to the distributor via a very well insulated, high-voltage wire.

According to the structure style, the ignition system could be divided into the conventional breaker point type ignition system (in use since the early 1900s), the electronic ignition system (popular since the mid 1970s, Figure 7 – 2), and the distributorless ignition system (introduced in the mid 1980s, Figure 7 – 3). At present, the conventional breaker point type ignition system has become obsolete, while the electronic ignition system and the distributorless ignition system are widely used in the modern vehicle.

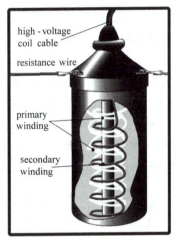

Figure 7 – 1 Internal structure diagram of ignition coil

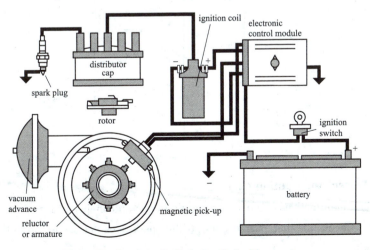

Figure 7 – 2 A typical electronic ignition system

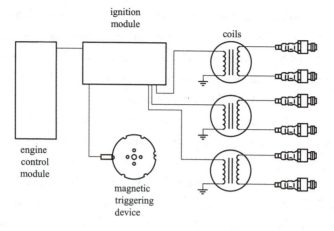

Figure 7 – 3 A typical distributorless ignition schematic

Toyota Corolla Repair Manual

Toyota Corolla 1.6 L adopts the distributorless ignition system (Figure 7 – 4). The spark plugs are fired directly from the coils. The ignition timing is controlled by an ignition control unit (ICU) and the engine control unit (ECU). The distributorless ignition system may have one coil per cylinder, or one coil for each pair of cylinders. Now, we introduce part of the service procedures of the ignition system.

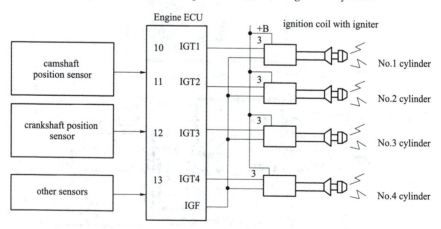

Figure 7 – 4 The distributorless ignition system of Toyota Corolla 1.6 L

1. Inspect the Ignition Coil

When malfunctions occur in the ignition coils and their circuitry:

(1) Check that the spark occurs. If the spark does not occur, go to the fourth step as follows.

Task 7 Ignition System Service Manual 53

(2) Check the wirings and the connectors between the engine ignition coils and the ECU. Disconnecting the connectors from the ECU, check the resistance between the engine ECU side wire connector terminal 25 (IGF) and the ignition coil wire side connector terminal 2 (IGF), and the resistor should be less than 1 Ω; check the resistance between the engine ECU side wire connector terminal 25 and terminal 17 (E1), and the resistor should exceed 1 MΩ; otherwise, repair or replace the wirings and the connectors.

(3) Check the engine ECU. Disconnecting all ignition coils connectors, turn the ignition switch ON, then check the voltage between the engine ECU connector terminal 25 and terminal 17, the value should be 4.5 – 5.5 V; check the voltage separately between the engine ECU connector terminals 10, 11, 12, 13 and terminal 17, the value must be 0.1 – 2.5 V; if abnormal, repair or replace the engine ECU.

(4) Check the wirings and the connectors between the engine ignition coil and the ECU. Disconnecting the connectors from the ECU and all ignition coils connectors, check the resistance separately between the engine ECU side wire connector terminals 10 (IGT1) and the No. 1 ignition coil wire side connector terminal 3, the resistance between the engine ECU side wire connector terminal 11 (IGT2) and the No. 2 ignition coil wire side connector terminal 3, the resistance between the engine ECU side wire connector terminal 12 (IGT3) and the No. 3 ignition coil wire side connector terminal 3, and the resistance between the engine ECU side wire connector terminal 13 (IGT4) and the No. 4 ignition coil wire side connector terminal 3, and all of the resistors should be less than 1 Ω; check the resistance separately between the engine ECU side wire connector terminals 10, 11, 12, 13 and terminal 17 (E1), the value should exceed 1 MΩ; otherwise, repair or replace the wirings and the connectors.

(5) Check the wirings and the connectors of all ignition coils. Disconnecting all ignition coils connectors, turn the ignition switch ON, then check the voltage between each ignition coil connector terminal 1 (+B) and terminal 4 (GND), the value should be the battery's voltage; if abnormal, repair or replace these wirings and connectors.

2. Inspect the Crankshaft Position Sensor

(1) Using an ohmmeter, measure the resistance between CPS terminals. In the cold state, the resistor is 1,630 – 2,740 Ω; but if in the hot state, the resistor is 2,065 – 3,225 Ω. If the resistance is not as specified, the crankshaft position sensor should be replaced.

Notice

"Cold" and "Hot" on the above sentences express the temperatures of the coils themselves. "Cold" is from -10 ℃ to 50 ℃ and "Hot" is from 50 ℃ to 100 ℃.

(2) Check the wirings and the connectors between crank position sensors and the ECU. Disconnecting the CPS and engine ECU connectors, check the continuity exists between the engine ECU side wire connector terminal 16(NE+) and the crank position sensor wire side connector terminal 1, between the engine ECU side wire connector terminal 24(NE-) and the crank position sensor wire side connector terminal 2, the result should be continuity. Check the resistance separately between the engine ECU side wire connector terminals 16, 24 and terminal 17, the resistor should be more than 1 MΩ; otherwise, repair or replace the wirings and the connectors.

(3) Check whether the crankshaft position sensor has been installed firmly, or whether the signals gear is intact; if abnormal, replace the crankshaft position sensor.

New Words 生词

1. ignition [ɪɡˈnɪʃən] n. 点火, 点燃
2. combustible [kəmˈbʌstəbl] adj. 易燃的
3. transform [trænsˈfɔːm] v. 转换, 改变
4. distributor [disˈtribjutə] n. 分电器
5. condenser [kənˈdensə] n. 电容器
6. circuitry [ˈsəːkitri] n. 线路
7. wrap [ræp] vt. 包; 缠绕
8. winding [ˈwaɪndɪŋ] n. 线圈
9. electromagnet [ɪˈlektrəʊmæɡnət] n. <物> 电磁体, 电磁铁
10. magnetic [mæɡˈnetɪk] adj 磁性的
11. engulf [ɪnˈɡʌlf] vt. 包住; 吞没
12. connector [kəˈnektə(r)] n. 连接器
13. terminal [ˈtəːminl] n. 端子, 接线柱
14. resistor [riˈzistə] n. 电阻
15. crankshaft [ˈkræŋkʃɑːft] n. 曲轴
16. intact [inˈtækt] adj. 完整无缺的
17. continuity [ˌkɒntiˈnjuː(ː)iti] n. 连续, 导通
18. abnormal [æbˈnɔːməl] adj. 反常的, 变态的

Phrases and Expressions 短语与表达

1. high-voltage spark 高压火花
2. ignition coil 点火线圈

Task 7 Ignition System Service Manual

3. ignition switch　　　　　　　　　　点火开关
4. spark plug　　　　　　　　　　　　火花塞
5. distributor cap　　　　　　　　　　分电器盖
6. electronic ignition　　　　　　　　电子点火
7. vacuum advance　　　　　　　　　真空提前
8. crankshaft position sensor　　　　曲轴位置传感器
9. IGF（igniter）　　　　　　　　　　点火器
10. E1（engine ground）　　　　　　　发动机搭铁
11. IGT1（igniter 1）　　　　　　　　点火器1
12. IGT2（igniter 2）　　　　　　　　点火器2
13. IGT3（igniter 3）　　　　　　　　点火器3
14. IGT4（igniter 4）　　　　　　　　点火器4
15. GND（ground）　　　　　　　　　搭铁（接地）
16. NE＋（crankshaft position sensor）　曲轴位置传感器信号输入端
17. NE－（crankshaft position sensor）　曲轴位置传感器信号输出端
18. G2（distributor）　　　　　　　　分电器
19. G＋［distributor（crank angle）］　分电器（曲轴角度）

Classroom Activities 课堂活动

1. Translate the English words in Figure 7 – 1 to Figure 7 – 4 into Chinese, and share with classmates.（将图 7 – 1 ~ 图 7 – 4 中的英文单词翻译成中文, 并与同学们分享。）
2. Smart‐board words game. 电子白板游戏法: 应用交互式电子白板互动课堂工具, 设计学习游戏, 让学生在游戏中训练单词。
   Image-matching activity.（图片与英文词汇匹配游戏。）（游戏操作方法及截屏说明在信息化教学教案里; 动态的游戏课件在信息化教学资源文件夹里。）

Grammar Notes 语法注释

The function of an ignition system in the gasoline engine is to transform the voltage from the battery to high-tension voltage, and timely introduce the electricity into the engine cylinder in accordance with the work order of the engine cylinder to ignite the air-fuel mixture by spark, so that the engine can be started normally.

句中"in accordance with"是"与……一致, 依照"之意; "so that the engine can be started normally"是结果状语从句, 表示"以至于……"; "to transform the voltage…

introduce the electricity into the engine cylinder"整个句子是表语从句,其主语为"the function"。

全句可译为:汽油发动机中,点火系统的功能是将蓄电池的低压电转变成高压电,并按发动机气缸工作顺序适时地引入气缸,形成电火花点燃混合气,从而使发动机正常工作。

Text Notes 课文注释

1. According to the structure style, the ignition system could be divided into the conventional breaker point type ignition system (in use since the early 1900s), the electronic ignition system (popular since the mid 1970s, Figure 7-2), and the distributorless ignition system (introduced in the mid 1980s, Figure 7-3).
点火系统按结构类型分为传统的触点式点火系统(从 20 世纪初开始使用)、电子点火系统(于 20 世纪 70 年代中期起开始受欢迎,图 7-2)和无分电器的点火系统(于 20 世纪 80 年代中期起开始被引入,图 7-3)。

2. The ignition timing is controlled by an ignition control unit (ICU) and the engine control unit (ECU).
点火控制单元与发动机的控制单元共同控制点火时间。

3. Disconnecting all ignition coils connectors, turn the ignition switch ON, then check the voltage between the engine ECU connector terminal 25 and terminal 17, the value should be 4.5-5.5 V; check the voltage separately between the engine ECU connector terminals 10,11,12,13 and terminal 17, the value must be 0.1-2.5 V; if abnormal, repair or replace the engine ECU.
拔下各点火线圈连接器,将点火开关转至"ON"位置,检测发动机 ECU 连接器端子 25 与端子 17 之间的电压,电压值应为 4.5~5.5 V;分别检测发动机 ECU 端子 10,11,12,13 与端子 17 之间的电压,均应为 0.1~2.5 V,否则应修理或更换发动机 ECU。

4. If the resistance is not as specified, the crankshaft position sensor should be replaced.
若测量出的电阻值与指定值不一致,就必须更换曲轴位置传感器。

Safety Tips 安全提示

为了避免人员伤害或损坏燃油喷射系统及点火系统,在进行点火线圈及其点火器线路的检测时,应注意以下安全事项:

Task 7　Ignition System Service Manual

（1）发动机运转或用起动机拖动发动机运转时，不要触摸或拔下点火线。

（2）连接或拔下点火系统及燃油喷射系统导线和检测仪接线前应关闭点火开关。

（3）如需用起动机拖动发动机运转而不起动发动机，则拔下点火线圈及喷油器的插头。

（4）清洗发动机之前必须关闭点火开关。

Exercises 练习

Part I　Choose the best answers from the following choices according to the reading material.

Car Ignition-Repairing and Maintenance Safety Tips

WAIT! — Not feeling well? Feeling tired and sleepy? So don't try to do repair work because you may get hurt. Don't work underneath the vehicle if you are not physically able — let the work beside. Work only when you are feeling well because work is not as important as you are.

Be careful — do not smoke when working near any fuel containing part, it may catch fire and can cause a big accident. If you have to smoke, if you really want to do it, do it before or after work.

While working with parts that contain fuel, then always keep a fire extinguisher nearby. Before starting work on the car, notify someone in your home you're about to do so, and give them an emergency number in case anything goes wrong.

Always be careful and cautious while working near battery — it may catch fire. Don't try to weld parts near battery with bare hands because it may burn or damage your skin.

Are you planning to work under the vehicle? Don't attempt repairing or applying maintenance work under a vehicle that's not supported properly. Keep your working environment as safe as possible, and make sure that your vehicle is supported properly. Secondly, keep someone beside you for help while working underneath the car, only then can you begin working.

It is very dangerous to work underneath a vehicle, whether it is your car or other vehicle. Always wear helmet while working underneath the vehicle. It can protect your head from any uncertainty and also from minor scratches.

1. Don't work _____ the vehicle if you are not physically able.

　　A. over　　　　B. underneath　　　　C. underside　　　　D. inside

2. If you _____ smoke, if you really want to do it, do it before or after work.
    A. want to   B. need   C. have to   D. wish
3. While working with parts that contain fuel, then always keep a _____ nearby.
    A. fire extinguisher   B. dustbin
    C. ashtray   D. box
4. Don't _____ repairing or applying maintenance work under a vehicle that's not supported properly.
    A. attend   B. attempt   C. try   D. intention
5. Don't try to weld parts near battery with _____ hands because it may burn or damage your skin.
    A. bald   B. naked   C. nude   D. bare
6. It is very _____ to work underneath a vehicle, whether it is your car or other vehicle.
    A. perilous   B. risky   C. dangerous   D. hazardous

Part II Translate the following into Chinese.
1. high-voltage spark   2. ignition coil
3. crankshaft position sensor   4. vacuum advance
5. engine control module   6. emergency brake
7. trouble code   8. fuel pump

Part III Translate the following into English.
1. 点火开关   2. 传动齿轮
3. 位置传感器   4. 分电器
5. 火花塞   6. 初级线圈

Part IV Translate the following sentences into Chinese.
1. The conventional ignition system consists of the battery, the ignition coil, the distributor, the condenser, the ignition switch, the spark plugs, the resistor and the necessary low and high tension wiring.
2. At present, the conventional breaker point type ignition system has become obsolete, while the electronic ignition system and the distributorless ignition system are widely used in the modern vehicle.
3. The distributorless ignition system may have one coil per cylinder, or one coil for each pair of cylinders.
4. Check the wirings and the connectors between the engine ignition coil and the ECU.

Task 7　Ignition System Service Manual　59

5. If the resistance is not as specified, the crankshaft position sensor should be replaced.

Part V　Complete the following questions based on the graphs below.

1. The typical ignition system is triggered by the primary ignition system. Please indicate the service's names as the chart below shows.

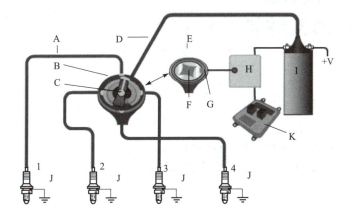

2. The electrical signal is generated by CKP, CAS. Write its name according to "CKP" abbreviation. How to calculate spark timing (See the chart below)?

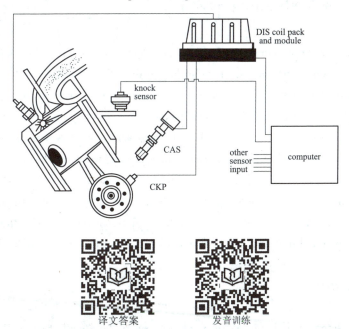

Task 8

Starting System Service Procedures
起动系统检测维修

学习目标:
1. 掌握起动系统的专业术语(英文);
2. 熟悉起动系统常见故障及检测维修方法。

 Text 课文

 Engine Starting System

The "starting system," the heart of the electrical system in your car, begins with the battery. When you turn the ignition key to the "Start" position, the battery voltage goes through the starting control circuit and activates the starter solenoid, which in turn energizes the starter motor. The starter motor cranks the engine.

A starter can only be operated when the automatic transmission shifter is in "Park" or "Neutral" position or if the car has a manual transmission, when the clutch pedal is depressed.

To accomplish this, there is a neutral safety switch installed at the automatic transmission (or at the clutch pedal). When the automatic transmission is not in "Park" or "Neutral" (or when the clutch pedal is not depressed), the neutral safety switch is open and the starter relay disconnects the starter control circuit (Figure 8-1).

Battery

The automotive battery, also known as a lead-acid storage battery, is an electrochemical device that produces voltage and delivers current. In an automotive battery we can reverse the electrochemical action, thereby recharging the battery, which

Task 8 Starting System Service Procedures 61

will then give us many years of service. The purpose of the battery is to supply current to the starter motor, and provide current to the ignition system while cranking, to supply additional current when the demand is higher than the alternator can supply and to act as an electrical reservoir.

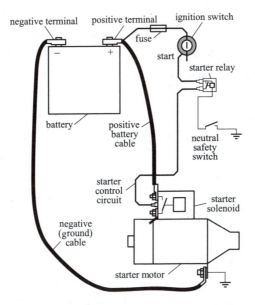

Figure 8 – 1 The simplified diagram of a typical starting system

Ignition Switch

The ignition switch allows the driver to distribute electrical current to where it is needed. There are generally 5 key switch positions that are used.

(1) Lock — All circuits are open (no current supplied) and the steering wheel is in the lock position. In some cars, the transmission lever cannot be moved in this position. If the steering wheel is applying pressure to the locking mechanism, the key might be hard to turn. If you do experience this type of condition, try moving the steering wheel to remove the pressure as you turn the key.

(2) Off — All circuits are open, but the steering wheel can be turned and the key cannot be extracted.

(3) Run — All circuits, except the starter circuit, are closed (current is allowed to pass through). Current is supplied to all but the starter circuit.

(4) Start — Power is supplied to the ignition circuit and the starter motor only. That is why the radio stops playing in the start position. This position of the ignition switch is spring loaded so that the starter is not engaged while the engine is running. This

position is used momentarily, just to activate the starter.

(5) Accessory — Power is supplied to all but the ignition and starter circuit. This allows you to play the radio, work the power windows, etc. while the engine is not running.

Neutral Safety Switch

This switch opens (denies current to) the starter circuit when the transmission is in any gear but Neutral or Park on automatic transmissions. This switch is normally connected to the transmission linkage or directly on the transmission. Most cars utilize this same switch to apply current to the back up lights when the transmission is put in reverse. Manual transmission cars will connect this switch to the clutch pedal so that the starter will not engage unless the clutch pedal is depressed. If you find that you have to move the shifter away from Park or Neutral to get the car to start, it usually means that this switch needs adjustment. If your car has an automatic parking brake release, the neutral safety switch will control that function also.

Starter Relay

A relay is a device that allows a small amount of electrical current to control a large amount of current. An automobile starter uses a large amount of current (250 + amps) to start an engine. If we were to allow that much current to go through the ignition switch, we would not only need a very large switch, but all the wires would have to be the size of battery cables (not very practical). A starter relay is installed in series between the battery and the starter. Some cars use a starter solenoid to accomplish the same purpose of allowing a small amount of current from the ignition switch to control a high current flow from the battery to the starter. The starter solenoid in some cases also mechanically engages the starter gear with the engine.

Battery Cable

Battery cables are large diameter, multi-stranded wire which carry the high current (250 + amps) necessary to operate the starter motor. Some have a smaller wire soldered to the terminal which is used to either operate a smaller device or to provide an additional ground. When the smaller cable burns, this indicates a high resistance in the heavy cable. Care must be taken to keep the battery cable ends (terminals) clean and tight. Battery cables can be replaced with ones that are slightly larger but never smaller.

Task 8 Starting System Service Procedures 63

Starter Motor

The starter motor is a powerful electric motor, with a small gear (pinion) attached to the end. When activated, the gear is meshed with a larger gear (ring), which is attached to the engine. The starter motor then spins the engine over so that the piston can draw in a fuel/air mixture, which is then ignited to start the engine. When the engine starts to spin faster than the starter, a device called an overrunning clutch automatically disengages the starter gear from the engine gear.

 ## Troubleshooting Basic Starting System Problems

Many starting system problems are the result of neglect. Table 8 – 1 will show you which problems you can fix yourself and which require professional service.

Table 8 – 1 The starting system problems, their causes and the ways to solve them

Problems	Causes	What to Do
The engine does not crank (The solenoid or relay does not click)	Dead battery	Charge or replace battery
	Loose, corroded or broken connections	Clean or repair connections
	Corroded battery terminals (lights will usually light)	Clean terminals
	Faulty ignition switch	Have the ignition switch checked/replaced
	Faulty neutral safety switch or clutch switch (To test: push on brake pedal, hold key in Start position and move the shift lever or clutch pedal)	Have neutral safety switch or clutch switch checked or replaced
	Defective starter switch, relay or solenoid	Have the defective components replaced
The engine will not crank (The solenoid or relay clicks)	Low or "dead" battery	Charge or replace the battery
	Corroded battery terminals or cables	Clean or replace the terminals or cables
	Defective starter solenoid or relay	Have defective components replaced
	Defective starter motor (if current is passed through the relay or solenoid)	Have the starter replaced or overhauled

continued

Problems	Causes	What to Do
The starter motor cranks slowly	Low battery	Charge or replace the battery
	Loose, corroded or broken connections	Clean, repair or replace the connections
	Cable size too small	Replace with proper size cables
	Internal starter motor problems	Have the starter replaced or overhauled
	Engine oil too heavy	Use proper oil viscosity for temperature
	Ignition timing too far advanced	Set timing to the specifications
Starter spins, but will not crank the engine	Broken starter drive gear	Have the drive gear replaced
	Broken flywheel teeth	Have the flywheel checked
Noisy starter motor	Starter mounting loose	Tighten the mounting bolts
	Worn starter drive gear or flywheel teeth	Have the starter or flywheel checked
	Worn starter bushings	Have the starter replaced or overhauled

New Words 生词

1. crank [kræŋk] v. 起动,转动曲柄
2. electrochemical [iˌlektrəuˈkemikəl] adj. 电化学的
3. alternator [ˈɔːltə(ː)neitə] n. 交流发电机
4. meshed [ˈmeʃt; məˈʃed] adj. 啮合的
5. spin [spin] v. 旋转
6. overhaul [ˌəuvəˈhɔːl] v. 彻底检查
7. energize [ˈenədʒaiz] v. 给予……电压,激活
8. disconnect [ˌdiskəˈnekt] v. 断开
9. reverse [riˈvəːs] v. 逆向(充电),倒转
10. distribute [disˈtribju(ː)t] v. 分发,分配
11. extract [iksˈtrækt] v. 拔出
12. mount [maunt] v. 安装
13. gear [giə] n. 齿轮 v. 调整,啮合,换挡
14. defective [diˈfektiv] adj. 有缺陷的,有问题的
15. accessory [ækˈsesəri] n. 附件

Task 8 Starting System Service Procedures   65

➡ Phrases and Expressions 短语与表达

1. starter solenoid	起动机电磁阀
2. starter relay	起动机继电器
3. clutch pedal	离合器踏板
4. neutral safety switch	空挡安全开关
5. starter motor	起动马达
6. electrical reservoir	蓄电池
7. multi-stranded wire	多股电线
8. oil viscosity	机油黏度
9. ignition timing too far advanced	点火提前角过大
10. overrunning clutch	超速离合器
11. automatic transmission	自动变速器
12. manual transmission	手动变速器
13. park	驻车挡
14. lead-acid storage battery	铅酸蓄电池
15. steering wheel	方向盘
16. transmission lever	换挡手柄
17. neutral	空挡

◎ Classroom Activities 课堂活动

1. Translate the English words in Figure 8-1 into Chinese; share these words with your classmates. （将图 8-1 中的英文单词翻译成中文；并与同学们分享。）

2. Flashcard identification: Let the students try to match the English flashcards with the Chinese ones. （卡片识别：让同学们尝试英文卡片与中文卡片的匹配活动。）
Flashcards（卡片）：
starter 起动机, starter control circuit 起动控制电路, voltage 电压, battery 蓄电池, relay 继电器, fuse 熔断丝, manual transmission 手动变速器, automatic transmission 自动变速器, neutral safety switch 空挡安全开关, clutch pedal 离合器踏板, crank 曲柄/转动曲柄, solenoid 电磁阀, motor 电动机, positive cable 正极导线。

3. Scrambled Words Quiz Game. （单词重组游戏法。）
利用黑板，将被打乱了字母顺序的单词（Scrambled Word）重新组合，拼成一个正确的新单词（New word）（教学组织方法的说明在信息化教学教案里）。例如：
Choose a letter correctly to create a new word.

Scrambled Words	New Words
ytrbate	battery
toorm	
reartst	
geeinn	
tiavcaet	
galtove	

adlep
hciwst
llinats
laeyr

Grammar Notes 语法注释

Have the ignition switch checked/replaced.
该句是一个主动形式表示被动意义的特殊结构。"have sth. done"是"要请某人做某事"的意思。
全句可译为:请人检查或更换点火开关。

Text Notes 课文注释

1. A starter can only be operated when the automatic transmission shifter is in "Park" or "Neutral" position or if the car has a manual transmission, when the clutch pedal is depressed.
   只有当自动变速器在驻车挡或空挡时(若是手动变速器,则离合器断开时),起动机才能运转。
2. When the automatic transmission is not in "Park" or "Neutral" (or when the clutch pedal is not depressed), the neutral safety switch is open and the starter relay disconnects the starter control circuit.
   当自动变速器不在驻车挡或空挡(或离合器没断开)时,空挡安全开关断开,并且起动机继电器断开起动机控制电路。
3. Care must be taken to keep the battery cable ends (terminals) clean and tight.
   应对电源线定期保养,以保证电源线接线柱清洁且连接牢固。
4. When the engine starts to spin faster than the starter, a device called an overrunning clutch automatically disengages the starter gear from the engine gear.
   当发动机的转速超过起动电动机的转速时,超速离合器自动断开起动机齿轮与发动机齿轮的啮合。

Safety Tips 安全提示

　　1. 勿用敲打起动电动机的方法诊断起动电动机的驱动故障。敲击会使电刷、电枢和衬套易位。敲打后的电动机即使能运行,也只是暂时的。
　　2. 电池中的电解液含有硫酸。硫酸是一种腐蚀性极强的酸,会对人造成严重的伤害。加注电解液时一定要注意安全。
　　3. 禁止掩埋或焚烧酸性含铅废电池。
　　4. 电池无论新旧,都应放在室内,且保持良好的通风状况。
　　5. 工作时不应佩戴手套、戒指及其他首饰,因为它们可能会接触汽车电气系统或正在运转中的零部件。

Task 8　Starting System Service Procedures 67

Exercises 练习

Part I　Choose the best answers from the following choices according to the text.

1. This switch _____ the starter circuit when the transmission is in any gear but Neutral or Park on automatic transmissions.
   A. closes　　　　B. cuts off　　　　C. on　　　　D. opens
2. When the ignition switch on the "Run," all circuits, except the starter circuit, are _____.
   A. opened　　　　B. closed　　　　C. open　　　　D. in
3. The starter motor then _____ the engine over so that the piston can draw in a fuel/air mixture.
   A. draws　　　　B. pulls　　　　C. spins　　　　D. takes
4. In an automotive battery we can _____ the electrochemical action, thereby recharging the battery, which will then give us many years of service.
   A. reverse　　　　B. discharge　　　　C. run　　　　D. make
5. The purpose of the battery is to supply additional current when the demand is _____ than the alternator can supply and to act as an electrical reservoir.
   A. higher　　　　B. lower　　　　C. fewer　　　　D. high
6. A starter relay is installed in series between the battery and the _____.
   A. engine　　　　B. alternator　　　　C. key switch　　　　D. starter
7. When the engine starts to spin faster than the starter, a device called an overrunning clutch automatically _____ the starter gear from the engine gear.
   A. installs　　　　B. disengages　　　　C. joins　　　　D. links
8. The starter spins, but will not crank engine. Which causes that? _____.
   A. Ignition timing too far advanced　　　B. Starter mounting loose
   C. Internal starter motor problems　　　D. Broken starter drive gear
9. The starter solenoid _____ also mechanically engages the starter gear with the engine.
   A. always　　　　B. seldom　　　　C. in some cases　　　　D. suddenly
10. If we were to allow that much current to go through the ignition switch, we would _____ need a very large switch, but all the wires would have to be the size of battery cables.
    A. so　　　　B. only　　　　C. not only　　　　D. more

Part II　Translate the following into English.

1. 交流发电机　　　　　　　　2. 啮合
3. 超速离合器　　　　　　　　4. 铅酸蓄电池
5. 换挡手柄　　　　　　　　　6. 自动变速器
7. 起动机　　　　　　　　　　8. 点火开关
9. 断开　　　　　　　　　　　10. 起动机继电器

Part III Translate the following into Chinese.
1. defective   2. accessory
3. distribute   4. extract
5. energize   6. spin
7. starter solenoid   8. steering wheel
9. clutch pedal   10. neutral safety switch

Part IV Translate the following sentences into Chinese.
1. The "starting system," the heart of the electrical system in your car.
2. The automotive battery, also known as a lead-acid storage battery, is an electrochemical device that produces voltage and delivers current.
3. All circuits are open (no current supplied) and the steering wheel is in the lock position.
4. A relay is a device that allows a small amount of electrical current to control a large amount of current.
5. Care must be taken to keep the battery cable ends (terminals) clean and tight.
6. The starter motor is a powerful electric motor, with a small gear (pinion) attached to the end. When activated, the gear is meshed with a larger gear (ring), which is attached to the engine.
7. Have the neutral safety switch or clutch switch checked or replaced.
8. Worn starter drive gear or flywheel teeth.

Part V Complete the following questions based on the graphs below.
1. Place the names of the parts in the panes.

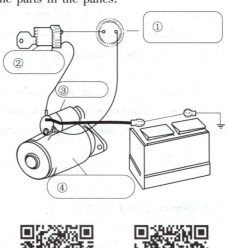

译文答案

发音训练

Task 9

Valvetronic Principles (BMW Service)
电子气门原理(宝马服务)

学习目标:
1. 掌握电子气门的组成、作用等的英文术语、词汇;
2. 能读懂电子气门的相关英文资料,并能进行中英文互译;
3. 能对电子气门的实物说出各组件的英文名称。

 Text 课文

 BMW's Valvetronic — Electronic Valve Technology

The solar term door can be divided into two types: namely traditional cable and electric wire. The former is to rely on the opening angle. When you pedal, the pull wire will shrink, so the other end of the solar term door will open. The deeper the pedal, the greater the throttle opening angle is, due to the use of a mechanical structure.

And more is the use of new electronic control system. Solar term door body part has a sensor. When you step on the accelerator, the sensor sends instructions to the solar term door body, the other side will control the opening angle according to the energy required by the engine. Some car dealers joined the Eco mode, they limit the opening angle to achieve the effect of fuel-efficient. Relative electric control system can also enhance the throttle sensitivity through movement mode.

Valvetronic is one of those terms often thrown around by BMW in their press releases, but seldom is being explained to the masses. We've all got accustomed to it without fully understanding how it works and what it really does for our cars and ultimately, for us.

Here is a nutshell what the valvetronic system is and how it works(Figure 9-1).

BMW's valvetronic system in the traditional gas phase institutions increased on a stick of eccentric shaft, a stepping motor and the middle push rod parts. Valvetronic is a variable valve timing system to offer continuous and precise control over variable intake valve lift and duration.

It typically works in conjunction with the independent Double VANO system that continuously varies the timing (on both intake and exhaust camshafts). Valvetronic - equipped engines rely on the amount of valve lift for load control, rather than a butter fly valve in the intake tract. In other words, in normal driving, the "gas pedal" controls the valvetronic hardware rather than the throttle plate.

Cylinder heads with valvetronic use an extra set of rocker arms, called intermediate arms (lift scaler), positioned between the valve stem and the camshaft.

These intermediate arms are able to pivot on a central point, by means of an extra, electronically actuated camshaft. This movement alone, without any movement of the intake camshaft, can vary the intake valves' lift from fully open, or maximum power, to almost closed, or idle.

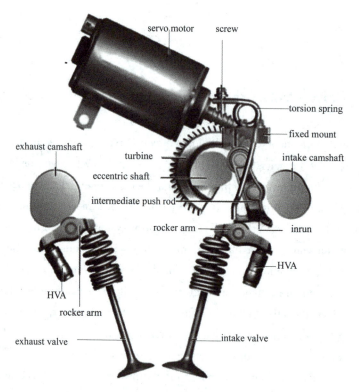

Figure 9 - 1 Variable valve lift system

Task 9 Valvetronic Principles (BMW Service)

New Words 生词

1. cable [ˈkeɪbl] n. 缆绳,电缆
2. pedal [ˈpedl] n. 踏板
3. throttle [ˈθrɒtl] n. 节流阀,风门
4. structure [ˈstrʌktʃə(r)] n. 结构,构造
5. enhance [ɪnˈhɑːns] v. 提高,加强,增加
6. gas [gæs] n. 气体,汽油
7. phase [feɪz] n. 相位,阶段
8. duration [djuˈreɪʃn] n. 持续,持续的时间,期间
9. pivot [ˈpɪvət] n. 枢轴,中心点,中心
10. idle [ˈaɪdl] n. 怠速

➡ Phrases and Expressions 短语与表达

1. solar term door	节气门
2. be divided into	被分成,分为
3. rely on	依靠,依赖
4. opening angle	开度角
5. cooperate with	合作,与合作
6. eccentric shaft	偏心轴
7. stepping motor	步进电动机
8. Eco mode	节能模式,环保模式
9. effect of fuel-efficient	节能效果
10. press release	新闻发布
11. gas phase institution	气相机构
12. BMW—Bavarian Motor Works	德国宝马汽车公司
13. VANOS(德语)	可变配气相位
14. HVA—hydraulic valve addition	液压气门补偿器
15. VVTS—variable-valve-timing system	可变气门正时系统
16. VVLS—variable valve lift system	可变气门升程机构

● **C**lassroom Activities 课堂活动

Translate the English words in Figure 9-1 into Chinese; share these words with your classmates. (将图 9-1 中的英文单词翻译成中文并与同学们分享。)

Grammar Notes 语法注释

It typically works in conjunction with the independent Double VVTS that continuously varies the timing (on both intake and exhaust camshafts).

句中的 in conjunction with 是固定搭配,"连同;配合;协力"的意思;"that continuously varies the timing"中,that引导定语从句,修饰VVTS。

全句译为:它通常配合独立的能持续改变进、排气凸轮轴的双可变气门正时系统一起工作。

Safety Tips 安全提示

为了避免人员伤害或损坏配气系统,在进行拆装时,应注意以下安全事项:

(1)工作前应检查所使用工具是否完好;工作时必须将工具摆放整齐,不得随地乱放;工作后应将工具清点检查并擦干净,按要求放入工具车或工具箱内。

(2)拆装零部件时,必须使用合适工具或专用工具,不得大力蛮干,不得用硬物手锤直接敲击零件。所有零件拆卸后要按顺序摆放整齐,不得随地堆放。

(3)转动发动机台架时,要注意安全,防止脱落;应缓慢转动,到位后将转动插销锁止。

Exercises 练习

Part I   Translate the following into English.

1. 电子气门   2. 气门升程
3. 负载   4. 油门踏板
5. 蝶阀   6. 持续时间
7. 节气门   8. 进气道

Part II   Translate the following into Chinese.

1. HVA   2. VANOS
3. Eco mode   4. gas phase institution
5. opening angle   6. hydraulic valve

Part III   Translate the following sentence into Chinese.

In other words, in normal driving, the "gas pedal" controls the valvetronic hardware rather than the throttle plate.

译文答案

发音训练

Task 10

Automatic Transmissions and Troubleshooting
自动变速箱及其故障排除

学习目标：
1. 掌握自动变速箱的专业英文词汇；
2. 熟悉汽车英语表达习惯；
3. 了解自动变速箱的组成、原理及故障排除方法。

 Text 课文

 Automatic Transmission Components

The main components that make up an automatic transmission include:

The planetary gear sets which are the mechanical systems that provide various forward gear ratios as well as reverse ones.

The hydraulic system which uses special transmission fluid sent under pressure by an oil pump through the valve body to control the clutches and the bands in order to control the planetary gear sets.

The seals and gaskets are used to keep the oil where it is supposed to be and prevented from leaking out.

The fluid torque converter which acts like a clutch to allow the vehicle to come to a stop in gear while the engine is still running.

The governor and the modulator or throttle cable that monitor speed and throttle position in order to determine when to shift.

On newer vehicles, shift points are controlled by computer which directs electrical solenoids to shift oil flow to the appropriate component at the right instant.

Fluid Torque Converter Operating

On automatic transmissions, the fluid torque converter takes the place of the clutch found on standard shift vehicles. It allows the engine to continue running when the vehicle comes to a stop.

As is shown in Figure 10-1, a fluid torque converter is a large doughnut shaped device (10 inches to 15 inches in diameter) that is mounted between the engine and the transmission. It consists of three internal elements that work together to transmit power to the transmission. The three elements of the torque converter are the pump, the turbine, and the stator. The pump is mounted directly to the converter housing which in turn is bolted directly to the engine's crankshaft and turns at the engine speed. The turbine is inside the housing and is connected directly to the input shaft of the transmission providing power to move the vehicle. The stator is mounted to a one-way clutch so that it can spin freely in one direction but not in the other. Each of the three elements has fins mounted in them to precisely direct the flow of oil through the converter.

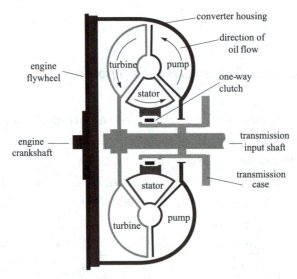

Figure 10-1 A fluid torque converter internal diagram

With the engine running, transmission fluid is pulled into the pump section and is pushed outward by centrifugal force until it reaches the turbine section which starts it turning. The fluid continues in a circular motion back towards the center of the turbine where it enters the stator. If the turbine is moving considerably slower than the pump, the fluid will make contact with the front of the stator fins which push the stator into the one-way clutch and prevent it from turning. With the stator stopped, the fluid is directed

Task 10 Automatic Transmissions and Troubleshooting   75

by the stator fins to re-enter the pump at a "helping" angle providing a torque increase. As the speed of the turbine catches up with the pump, the fluid starts hitting the stator blades on the back side causing the stator to turn in the same direction as the pump and turbine. As the speed increases, all three elements begin to turn at approximately the same speed.

Since the 1980s, in order to improve fuel economy, torque converters have been equipped with a lockup clutch (Figure 10 – 2) which locks the turbine to the pump as the vehicle speed reaches approximately 45 – 50 mph. This lockup is controlled by computer and usually won't engage unless the transmission is in 3rd or 4th gear.

Figure 10 – 2 A lock-up clutch

Computer Controls

The computer uses sensors on the engine and transmission to detect such things as throttle position, vehicle speed, engine speed, engine load, brake pedal position, etc. to control exact shift points as well as how soft or firm the shift should be. Once the computer receives this information, it then sends signals to a solenoid pack inside the transmission. The solenoid pack contains several electrically controlled solenoids that redirect the fluid to the appropriate clutch pack or servo in order to control shifting. Computerized transmissions even learn your driving style and constantly adapt to it so that every shift is timed precisely when you need it.

Removal of Components

To remove the automatic transmission components from your car, you will need a basic wrench set, socket set, jack stands, floor jack, and a transmission jack. You should do as follows.

(1) Raise both the front and rear of your car and support it on good quality jack stands.

(2) Remove the linkage/cables for the shifter and throttle valve/kick down.

(3) Remove the vacuum line for the modulator if so equipped.

(4) Remove the rear U-joint from the rear end and slide the driveshaft/yoke from the transmission. Place a rag or an old yoke on the rear of the transmission to prevent fluid from coming out.

(5) Remove the speedometer gear assembly.

(6) Place the transmission jack under the transmission pan and slightly lift the transmission.

(7) Remove the lower bell housing cover and remove the torque converter bolts.

(8) Remove the bell housing bolts.

(9) Remove the 4 cross member bolts and the rear transmission mount.

(10) Raise the transmission jack and remove the cross member.

(11) Roll the transmission jack to the rear of car while slowly lowering the transmission. Be sure to look and make certain that the transmission is clearing everything and nothing is attached that should not be.

Diagnosing and Troubleshooting

(1) The first thing you should do when you suspect any transmission problem is to check the transmission fluid level and condition. The engine should be running with the transmission in "PARK."

(2) If the fluid level is low, fill to the proper level and test the vehicle. If the abnormal symptoms are gone, the primary problem is a leak. Then continue to monitor the fluid level, add as appropriate, and have the leak source diagnosed before additional problems occur.

A slow leak is worse than a big leak! A slow leak will allow the transmission to operate until the level is low enough to subject the unit to low fluid operation which will cause excessive wear! A big leak will certainly get your attention and usually result in little or no internal damage.

(3) There are numerous transmission seals, gaskets, and O-rings that can leak. Therefore, a visual inspection is necessary to determine leak sources before an estimate for repair can be made.

Task 10 Automatic Transmissions and Troubleshooting

If the fluid level is okay, and you still have a problem:

Check for any transmission related linkage, vacuum hoses, or electrical connections that may be loose or disconnected. One of the most common problems is corroded battery terminal connections. Clean terminals are particularly important for late model computer controlled transmissions.

New Words 生词

1. troubleshooting [ˈtrʌblˌʃuːtiŋ] n. 故障诊断与排除
2. gasket [ˈɡæskit] n. 垫圈，衬垫
3. governor [ˈɡʌvənə] n. 管理者；调节器
4. modulator [ˈmɔdjuleitə] n. 调节器
5. solenoid [ˈsəulinɔid] n. 螺线管
6. pump [pʌmp] n. 泵
7. turbine [ˈtəːbin, -bain] n. 涡轮
8. stator [ˈsteitə] n. 定子，固定片
9. centrifugal [senˈtrifjuɡəl] adj. 离心的
10. doughnut [ˈdəunʌt] n. 圆环图
11. up-shift [ʌpʃift] v. 升挡，换高速挡
12. down-shift [daunʃift] v. 降挡，换低速挡
13. technician [tekˈnɪʃ(ə)n] n. 技术员，技师
14. symptom [ˈsimptəm] n. 症状，征兆
15. band [bænd] n. 带子，制动带

➡ Phrases and Expressions 短语与表达

1. automatic transmission   自动变速器
2. planetary gear set   行星齿轮组
3. transmission fluid   变速器油液
4. hydraulic system   液压系统
5. valve body   阀体
6. throttle cable   节气门拉线
7. shift point   换挡点
8. fluid torque converter   液力变矩[扭]器，转矩变换器
9. take the place of   代替
10. converter housing   变矩器壳体

11. one-way clutch	单向离合器
12. centrifugal force	离心力
13. mph(miles per hour)	时速(每小时所行驶之英里数)
14. sun gear	中心齿轮,太阳轮
15. ring gear	环形齿轮,齿圈
16. planet gear	行星齿轮
17. planet carrier	行星架
18. stick shift	顶杆挡
19. at will	随意,任意
20. wrench set	成套扳手
21. socket set	套筒组
22. jack stand	汽车台架(= car stand)
23. floor jack	底盘千斤顶,底盘支撑架
24. transmission jack	变速箱支撑架
25. lock-up clutch	锁止离合器

Classroom Activities 课堂活动

1. Translate the English words in Figure 10 – 1, Figure 10 – 2 into Chinese; share these words with your classmates. (将图 10 – 1 和图 10 – 2 中的英文单词翻译成中文, 并与同学们分享。)

2. Smart-board words game. 电子白板游戏法:应用交互式电子白板互动课堂工具,设计词汇与图片的匹配学习游戏,让学生们在游戏中得到词汇训练。
Image-matching activity(图片与英文词汇匹配游戏):移动英文词组到相应零件的框内,完成一组训练后点击 Check 键,可检查对错。(游戏操作方法及截屏说明,放在信息化教学教案里;动态的游戏课件与教案一起,均放在信息化教学资源文件夹里。)

Grammar Notes 语法注释

The hydraulic system which uses special transmission fluid sent under pressure by an oil pump through the valve body to control the clutches and the bands in order to control the planetary gear sets.

句中 which 引导一个定语从句, which 指代的是前面的 hydraulic system; sent 是过去分词做后置定语, 在这里相当于 which is sent, 修饰 transmission fluid。在书面语中经常可以看到过去分词做后置定语这种表达法, 因为它相对于从句来说简单且顺口, 在今后的写作中, 我们可以多模仿这种表达法代替定语从句; in order to 是个固

Task 10 Automatic Transmissions and Troubleshooting

定搭配,表示"为了……,用来……"。
全句可译为:液压系统采用在油泵压力下流经阀体的专用变速器油液来控制离合器和伺服带,以便控制行星齿轮组。

Text Notes 课文注释

1. A fluid torque converter is a large doughnut shaped device (10 inches to 15 inches in diameter) that is mounted between the engine and the transmission.
   液力变矩器是个大圆环状的装置,直径在 10~15 in.①,它被安装在发动机和变速箱之间。

2. The stator is mounted to a one-way clutch so that it can spin freely in one direction but not in the other.
   定子安装在一个单向离合器上,这样它只可以在一个方向上自由旋转。

3. If the turbine is moving considerably slower than the pump, the fluid will make contact with the front of the stator fins which push the stator into the one-way clutch and prevent it from turning.
   如果涡轮比泵轮运转得慢很多,那么自动变速器油液将会作用在定子散热片前端,从而推动定子到单向离合器中锁定。

4. Remove the speedometer gear assembly.
   拆下车速表齿轮总成。

5. If the fluid level is low, fill to the proper level and test the vehicle.
   如果自动变速器液液面过低,则要添加变速器液到合适位置并进行试车。

Safety Tips 安全提示

(1) 自动变速器轿车中的自动变速器是轿车关键的部件之一,每行驶 50 000 km 左右,必须依照厂家的建议,彻底清洗变速器或者更换油液。

(2) 自动变速器能使汽车发动机处于最佳工况,充分利用发动机功率,有利于降低排放污染,减小起步冲击,过载时还能起保护作用。它是由液力变矩器、齿轮机构、液压机构、湿式离合器和涡轮传动装置等部分组成的。这些机构都用同一种油液润滑和传递能量,这种专用液体称为汽车自动变速器油(ATF)。ATF 的主要作用是传递转矩,工作温度在 140 ℃ 左右。

(3) 维修人员在处理了发动机机油、差速器液体或变速器液体后,应用肥皂清洗双手,或在处理此类液体时戴上橡胶防护手套。

---

① 1 in. = 2.54 cm。

Exercises 练习

Part I　Choose the best answers from the following choices according to the text.

1. The major parts of the _____ include the transmission case, the input shaft, the output shaft, the countershaft, the driving gear, the transmission fork, etc.
   A. transmission   B. clutch
   C. catalytic converter   D. fuel filter

2. An automobile can get a smooth start when a power ratio is provided to multiply the _____ of the engine.
   A. centrifugal force   B. torque
   C. clamp force   D. holding capacity

3. The transmission is used to change the ratio between the _____ rpm and the driving wheel rpm.
   A. transmission   B. clutch   C. engine   D. catalytic converter

4. On automatic transmissions, the fluid torque converter takes the place of the _____ found on standard shift vehicles.
   A. clutch   B. manual transmission
   C. shifter   D. lever

5. The basic _____ consists of a sun gear, a ring gear and two or more planet gears, all remaining in constant mesh.
   A. clutch   B. automatic transmission
   C. engine   D. planetary gear set

6. Seals and _____ are used to keep the oil where it is supposed to be and prevented from leaking out.
   A. stators   B. pumps   C. bands   D. gaskets

7. The _____ which acts like a clutch to allow the vehicle to come to a stop in gear while the engine is still running.
   A. one-way clutch   B. fuel pressure regulator
   C. fluid torque converter D. air cleaner

8. The governor and the modulator or _____ monitor the speed and throttle position in order to determine when to shift.
   A. throttle cable   B. jack stand
   C. stick shift   D. wrench set

9. With the engine running, _____ is pulled into the pump section and is pushed outward by centrifugal force until it reaches the turbine section which starts it turning.
   A. brake fluid   B. transmission fluid
   C. coolant   D. lubricating oil

10. The _____ is connected to the planet carrier which is also connected to a "multi-disk" clutch pack.
    A. input shaft   B. countershaft   C. output shaft   D. planet gear

Task 10 Automatic Transmissions and Troubleshooting

Part II   Translate the following into English.

1. 成套扳手   2. 中心齿轮
3. 变速箱支撑架   4. 离心力
5. 阀体   6. 行星架
7. 液压系统   8. 自动变速器
9. 行星齿轮组   10. 环形齿轮

Part III   Translate the following into Chinese.

1. transmission fluid   2. planet gear
3. stick shift   4. fluid torque converter
5. one-way clutch   6. floor jack
7. shift point   8. converter housing
9. socket set   10. jack stand

Part IV   Translate the following sentences into Chinese.

1. If the turbine is moving considerably slower than the pump, the fluid will make contact with the front of the stator fins which push the stator into the one-way clutch and prevent it from turning.
2. If the fluid level is low, fill to the proper level and test the vehicle.
3. The stator is mounted to a one-way clutch so that it can spin freely in one direction but not in the other.
4. A fluid torque converter is a large doughnut shaped device that is mounted between the engine and the transmission.
5. A transmission is a speed and power changing device installed at some point between the engine and the driving wheels of the vehicle.
6. Place the transmission jack under the transmission pan and slightly lift the transmission.
7. Another advantage of these "smart" transmissions is that they have a self-diagnostic mode which can detect a problem early on and warn you with an indicator light on the dash.

译文答案

发音训练

Task 11

Brake System Service Manual
制动系统维修手册

学习目标:
1. 掌握制动系统的专业英文词汇;
2. 能读懂英文版的制动系统维修手册;
3. 能理解防抱死制动系统故障识别码的读取。

 Text 课文

Brake System

The brake system is the most important system in cars. If the brakes fail, the result can be disastrous. Brakes are actually energy conversion devices, which convert the kinetic energy (momentum) of the vehicle into heat energy. When stepping on the brakes, the driver commands a stopping force ten times as powerful as the force that puts the car in motion. The brake system can exert thousands of pounds of pressure on each of the four brakes.

As is shown in Figure 11-1, the brake system is composed of the following basic components: The "master cylinder," which is located under the hood, and is directly connected to the brake pedal, converts driver's foot's mechanical pressure into hydraulic pressure. Steel "brake lines" and flexible "brake hoses" connect the master cylinder to the "slave cylinders" located at each wheel. Brake fluid, specially designed to work in extreme conditions, fills the system. "Shoes" and "Pads" are pushed by the slave cylinders to contact the "drum" and "rotors" thus causing drag, which (hopefully) slows the car.

The typical brake system consists of disk brakes in front and either disk or drum brakes in the rear connected by a system of tubes and hoses that link the brake at each wheel to the master cylinder.

Task 11 Brake System Service Manual

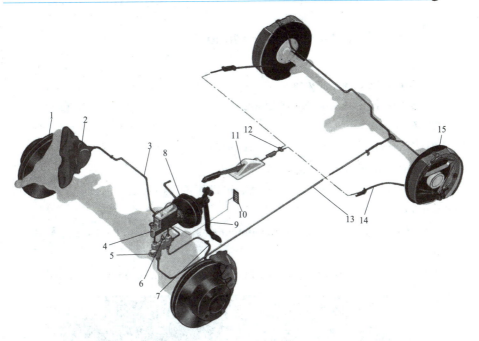

Figure 11 –1   A brake system

1 – front brake disc; 2 – caliper assy, front brake; 3 – brake line, RF;
4 – master cylinder; 5 – combination brake switch; 6 – brake warning switch;
7 – brake line, LF; 8 – vacuum booster; 9 – brake pedal; 10 – brake warning lamp;
11 – parking brake lever; 12 – equalizer; 13 – rear brake line; 14 – parking brake cable; 15 – rear brake assy.

The arrangement of the braking system on the vehicle is shown in Figure 11 – 2.

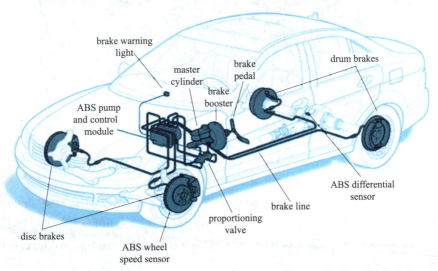

Figure 11 – 2   The arrangement of the braking system on the vehicle

Honda CR – V Repair Manual

1. Hydraulic Brake System

1) Brake Hoses and Steel Lines

To Remove:

(1) Disconnect the negative battery cable.

(2) Raise and safely support the vehicle.

(3) Remove any wheel and tire assemblies necessary for access to the particular line you are removing.

(4) Thoroughly clean the surrounding area at the joints to be disconnected (Figure 11 – 3).

(5) Place a suitable drain pan under the connection to be disconnected.

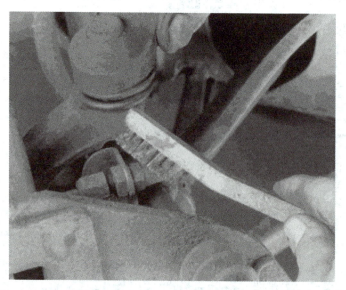

Figure 11 – 3 Using a brush to clean the fittings of any debris

(6) By using two line wrenches (one to hold the connection and the other to turn the fitting), disconnect the hose or line to be replaced.

(7) Disconnect the other end of the line or hose, moving the drain pan if necessary. Always use a line wrench to avoid damaging the fitting.

(8) Disconnect any retaining clips or brackets holding the line and remove the line from the vehicle.

To Install:

Install the new line or hose, starting with the end farthest from the master cylinder.

Connect the other end, and then confirm that both fittings are correctly threaded and turn smoothly using finger pressure. Make sure the new line will not rub against any other part. Brake lines must be at least 1/2 in (13 mm) from the steering column and other moving parts. Any protective shielding or insulators must be reinstalled in the original location.

2) **Master Cylinder**

CAUTION: Do not spill brake fluid on the vehicle; it may damage the paint; if brake fluid does contact the paint, wash it off immediately with water.

To Remove:

(1) Remove the air cleaner assembly.

(2) Release the engine wire harness clips on the strut brace, and remove the strut brace.

(3) With M/T: Remove the clutch reservoir bracket from the strut brace, and move it aside. Do not disconnect the clutch hose from the reservoir.

(4) Disconnect the brake fluid level sensor connector.

(5) Remove the clutch reservoir and engine wire harness clip from the master cylinder mounting base.

(6) Remove the reservoir cap and brake fluid from the reservoir.

(7) Remove the reservoir on the master cylinder mounting base.

(8) Disconnect the brake lines from the master cylinder.

(9) Remove the master cylinder mounting nuts and washers.

(10) Remove the master cylinder from the brake booster.

(11) Remove the rod seal from the master cylinder.

To Install:

(1) Install the rod seal on the master cylinder.

(2) Check the pushrod clearance before installing the master cylinder.

(3) Install the master cylinder on the brake booster.

(4) Install the master cylinder mounting nuts and washers.

(5) Connect the brake lines to the master cylinder.

(6) Install the reservoir on the master cylinder mounting base.

(7) Bleed the brake system.

(8) Fill the reservoir with brake fluid and install the reservoir cap.

(9) Install the strut brace.

(10) Install engine wire harness clips on the strut brace.

(11) Connect the brake fluid level sensor connector.

(12) Install the air cleaner assembly.

2. Disc Brakes (Figure 11-4)

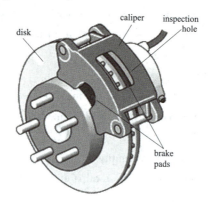

Figure 11-4 A disc brake

Brake Caliper
To Disassemble:

(1) Remove the caliper from the vehicle and place it on a clean workbench.

Note: Depending upon the vehicle, there are two different procedures to remove the piston from the caliper. Refer to the brake pad replacement procedure to make sure you have the correct procedure for your vehicle.

(2) Use a tool to remove the caliper boot, being careful not to scratch the housing bore.

(3) Remove the piston seals from the groove in the caliper bore.

(4) Carefully remove the brake bleeder valve cap and valve from the caliper housing.

(5) Inspect the caliper bores, pistons and mounting threads for scoring or excessive wear.

(6) Use crocus cloth to polish out light corrosion from the piston and bore.

(7) Clean all parts with denatured alcohol and dry with compressed air.

To Assemble:

(1) Lubricate and install the bleeder valve and cap.

(2) Install the new seals into the caliper bore grooves, making sure they are not twisted.

(3) Lubricate the piston bore.

(4) Install the pistons and boots into the bores of the calipers and push to the bottom of the bores.

(5) Use a suitable installer to seat the boots in the housing (Figure 11-5).

Task 11 Brake System Service Manual

Figure 11 – 5   Installing the boot

(6) Install the caliper in the vehicle.

(7) Install the wheel and tire assembly, then carefully lower the vehicle.

(8) Properly bleed the brake system.

3. ABS

Stopping a car in a hurry on a slippery road can be very challenging. Anti-lock braking systems (ABS) take a lot of challenge out of this occasional nerve-wracking event. In fact, on slippery surfaces, even professional drivers can't stop as quickly without an ABS as an average driver can with an ABS. Figure 11 – 6 shows the location of anti-lock brake components.

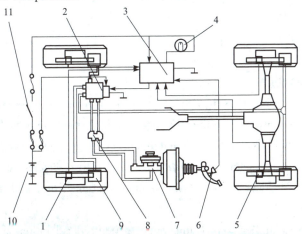

Figure 11 – 6   Location of anti-lock brake components

1 – the fore tire speed sensor; 2 – brake pressure regulator; 3 – anti-lock system electronic control unit;

4 – anti-lock system warning lamp; 5 – the rear tire speed sensor; 6 – parking lamp switch;

7 – master cylinder; 8 – proportioning valve; 9 – wheel cylinder; 10 – storage battery; 11 – ignition switch

There are four main components in an ABS:
- Speed sensor
- Valve
- Pump
- Controller

1) **Speed Sensor**

The anti-lock braking system needs some way of knowing when a wheel is about to lock up. The speed sensors, which are located at each wheel, or in some cases in the differential, provide this information.

2) **Valve**

There is a valve in the brake line of each brake controlled by the ABS. In some systems, the valve has three positions.

In position one, the valve is open; the pressure from the master cylinder is passed right through to the brake.

In position two, the valve blocks the line, isolating that brake from the master cylinder. This prevents the pressure from rising further should the driver push the brake pedal harder.

In position three, the valve releases some of the pressure from the brake.

3) **Pump**

Since the valve is able to release pressure from the brakes, there has to be some way to put that pressure back. That is what the pump does; when a valve reduces the pressure in a line, the pump is there to get the pressure back up.

4) **Controller**

The controller is a computer in the car. It watches the speed sensors and controls the valves.

ABS Operation

The controller monitors the speed sensors at all times. It is looking for decelerations in the wheel that are out of the ordinary. Right before the wheel locks up, it will experience a rapid deceleration. If left unchecked, the wheel would stop much more quickly than any car could. It might take a car five seconds to stop from 60 mph (96.6 kph) under ideal conditions, but a wheel that locks up could stop spinning in less than a second.

The ABS controller knows that such a rapid deceleration is impossible, so it reduces the pressure to that brake until it sees acceleration, then it increases the pressure until it sees the deceleration again. It can do this very quickly, before the tire can actually significantly change speed. The result is that the tire slows down at the same rate as the car, with the brakes keeping the tires very near the point at which they will start to lock up. This gives the system maximum braking power.

When the ABS system is in operation, you will feel a pulsing in the brake pedal; this comes from the rapid opening and closing of the valves. Some ABSs can cycle up to 15 times per second.

4. ABS's DTC Identification

There are two ways to show ABS's DTC: the "ABS" light on the dashboard and the LED light on the ECU.

1) Read DTC Through the "ABS" Light

DTC Reading:

(1) Turn the ignition switch to OFF position.

(2) Use SCS cross-wiring to short out glove box.

(3) Turn the ignition switch to ON position.

(4) Read light flashes and output DTC by using instrument "ABS."

DTC Removal:

(1) Turn the ignition switch to OFF position.

(2) Remove SCS cross-wiring.

(3) Remove the ABS fuse in relay box and connect it after 10 s, then DTC can be removed.

Note: Some vehicles with the slightly different procedures: unplug fuse to remove DTC first, and then remove SCS cross-wiring.

2) Read DTC Through LED Lights on ECU

DTC Reading:

(1) Turn the ignition switch to ON position, but do not start the engine.

(2) The ABS LED lights on ECU flash after 10 seconds, then they can read DTC.

DTC Removal:

With troubleshooting, ABS ECU Connector is removed for more than 15 s to eliminate DTC, and then connect it.

Always follow diagnostic trouble codes chart to correct trouble.

New Words 生词

1. disastrous [di'zɑːstrəs] adj. 灾难性的,损失惨重的,悲伤的

2. negative ['negətiv] adj. 否定的,消极的,负的,阴性的

3. fitting [ˈfitiŋ] adj. 适合的,相称的,适宜的 n. 试穿,试衣,装配,装置
4. insulator [ˈinsjuleitə(r)] n. 绝缘体,绝热器
5. booster [ˈbuːstə] n. 助力器,增强器,放大器
6. caliper [ˈkælipə] n. 测径器,卡钳 v. 用卡钳测量
7. pad [pæd] n. 垫,衬垫,便笺簿
8. pivot [ˈpivət] n. 枢轴 v. 旋转
9. deterioration [diˌtiəriəˈreiʃən] n. 变坏,退化,堕落
10. retainer [riˈteinə] n. [机]固定器,护圈,护管
11. inhalation [ˌinhəˈleiʃən] n. 吸入
12. nerve-wracking [ˈnəːvˌrækiŋ] adj. 极端令人头疼的(= nerve-racking)
13. pulsing [ˈpʌlsiŋ] n. 脉冲,脉冲的产生,脉动
14. eliminate [iˈlimineit] v. 排除,消除

➡ Phrases and Expressions 短语与表达

1. kinetic energy 动能
2. heat energy 热能
3. in motion 在运转中,处于兴奋状态
4. master cylinder 主缸
5. slave cylinder 从动缸
6. brake hose 制动软管
7. hydraulic brake system 液压制动系统
8. protective shielding 防护屏,护板
9. air cleaner 空气过滤器
10. wire harness 束线
11. strut brace 支柱,压杆(= strut bracing)
12. brake fluid level sensor 制动液位传感器
13. reservoir cap 容器盖,储蓄器盖
14. brake fluid 制动液
15. rod seal 杆密封
16. pushrod clearance 推杆间隙
17. brake booster 制动助力器
18. brake caliper 制动钳
19. depend upon 依赖,依靠(= depend on)

Task 11 Brake System Service Manual

20. caliper boot	（卡）钳保护罩
21. brake bleeder valve cap	制动液排放盖
22. brake pad	制动块
23. flange bolt	凸缘螺栓
24. brake disc	制动盘
25. regardless of	忽略，不管，不顾
26. be hazardous to	冒险，危险
27. parking brake	驻车制动(器)
28. brake shoe	制动蹄
29. brake cable	制动绳索
30. brake equalizer	制动平衡臂，游动杠杆
31. anti-lock braking system	防抱制动系统(= ABS)
32. lock up	锁止
33. kph	千米/时(= kilometers per hour)

Classroom Activities 课堂活动

Translate the English words in Figure 11 – 1, Figure 11 – 2 into Chinese, and share with your classmates. （将图 11 – 1、图 11 – 2 中的英文单词翻译成中文，并与同学们分享。）

Grammar Notes 语法注释

The typical brake system consists of disk brakes in front and either disk or drum brakes in the rear connected by a system of tubes and hoses that link the brake at each wheel to the master cylinder.

consist of 是个固定短语，表示"由……组成，包含……"；connected 是过去分词做后置定语，相当于"which is connected…"，这种表达法在平时经常可以见到，大家要认真体会；句中 that 引导的定语从句修饰"tubes and hoses"；link… to… 表示"连接……和……"。

全句可译为：典型的制动系统由前端的盘式制动器和后端的盘式或鼓式制动器组成，每个车轮的制动器通过一些管子和软管系统连接到工作主缸。

Text Notes 课文注释

1. The brake system is composed of the following basic components.

制动系统由以下基本部件组成。

2. "Shoes" and "pads" are pushed by the slave cylinders to contact the "drum" and "rotors" thus causing drag, which (hopefully) slows the car.

从动缸(的制动液)推动"(制动)蹄"和"(制动)块"与"(制动)鼓"和"(制动)转子"接触,从而产生对车辆减速的摩擦运动。

3. Disconnect the negative battery cable.

断开蓄电池负极端。

4. Connect the parking brake cable to the parking brake lever.

将驻车制动绳索连接到驻车制动杆。

5. In position one, the valve is open; the pressure from the master cylinder is passed right through to the brake.

在位置1上,阀门打开;主缸的压力完全传递到制动器上。

6. With troubleshooting, ABS ECU Connector is removed for more than 15s to eliminate DTC, and then connect it.

发现并修理故障后,断开防抱制动系统的电控单元连接器不少于15s以便清除诊断故障码,然后再将它连接起来。

Safety Tips 安全提示

(1) 汽车经过清洗或涉水,制动系统必然会潮湿,使摩擦系数变小,车轮制动力不均衡,结果造成汽车在制动时制动距离变长或制动偏向一边,从而造成行驶危险。欲使制动系统干燥,让汽车以安全速度行驶,就一面轻踩制动踏板,使制动系统发热,持续这样的动作,直到制动性能恢复正常为止。

(2) 为节省制动次数与防止制动器过热,在下坡前,先降低车速并换低速挡,以免降低制动性能。

(3) 旧的制动蹄和制动衬块应密封起来,以防止制动材料中的石棉纤维通过空气传播而危害人体。若石棉被弄湿,则可被看作一般的固体废物。

(4) 勿将制动液与废弃的发动机机油混合。

(5) 勿将制动液倒在排水沟中或地面上。

(6) 切勿使用压缩空气清洁制动器上的灰尘,细微的滑石粉状制动器灰尘也会对健康造成危害。

Exercises 练习

Part I Draw lines from the English words to their respective Chinese ones and read them correctly.

1. anti-lock brake system　　　　　　　　a) 制动主缸

2. the wheel speed sensor
3. the electrical control unit
4. instrument panel
5. lock up
6. rear-wheel drive
7. hydraulic actuator
8. driving stability
9. warning light
10. magnetic induction
11. shut down
12. shut off
13. solenoid valve
14. wheel cylinder
15. master cylinder
16. brake fluid
17. brake band
18. disc brake
19. heat energy
20. brake booster
21. single-piston floating caliper

b）制动助力器
c）警告灯
d）热能
e）盘式制动器
f）制动带
g）制动液
h）电磁阀
i）关闭,分离
j）停车,关闭
k）磁感应
l）操纵稳定性
m）液压执行机构
n）后轮驱动
o）锁住
p）仪表板
q）电子控制单元
r）车轮转速传感器
s）防抱死制动系统
t）制动轮缸
u）单活塞浮钳盘式制动器

Part II   Write out the English names of the parts of the disc brake according to the figure below.

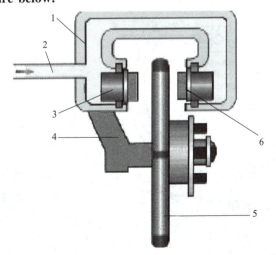

Part III Discuss the following questions in groups and write your answers on the white paper.

1. What are the true advantages of the ABS?
2. What are the main components of a disc brake?

Part IV Fill the missing words in the blanks of the following dialogue and role-play in pairs.

Mary: Hello, Rose, nice to see you.

Rose: Hello, Mary, nice to see you, too.

Mary: What did you major in in the university?

Rose: Well, I majored in automobile engineering.

Mary: Oh, I feel it is difficult to study. Can you explain the ABS to me?

Rose: Well, the ABS is the abbreviation of _____. It is designed to provide _____ during hard braking by adjusting the hydraulic pressure at each wheel to prevent wheel lockup.

Mary: Oh, it's very complex for me. What are the main components? What is the function of the final drive assembly?

Rose: The system's main components are _____, _____, and _____.

Part V Match the English phrases or words with the numbers in the figure below and write them down.

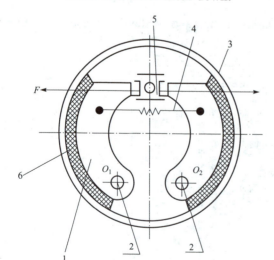

1. _____; 2. _____; 3. _____;
4. _____; 5. _____; 6. _____;

Task 11 Brake System Service Manual

Part VI   Translation.

1. The most efficient braking pressure takes place just before each wheel will lock up.
2. Anti-lock brake systems solve this lockup problem by rapidly pumping the brakes whenever the system detects a wheel that is locked up.
3. ABS wheel speed sensors are installed at each wheel, and they transmit wheel and tire speed information to the computer.
4. The rear-wheel ABS is designed to maintain directional stability and prevent the vehicle from skidding sideways in emergencies.
5. 现代汽车中常见的盘式制动器是浮钳盘式制动器。
6. 鼓式制动造价便宜,且容易与紧急制动机构配合。
7. 车轮防抱死制动系统具有自诊断功能。
8. 现代汽车后轮采用鼓式制动,前轮采用盘式制动。

译文答案

发音训练

Task 12

Power Steering System Services
动力转向系统检测维修

学习目标：

1. 掌握动力转向系统组成的英文术语、词汇；
2. 能读懂动力转向系统相关的英文资料，并能进行中英文互译；
3. 能根据动力转向系统维修的英文指示进行维修操作；
4. 能针对动力转向系统实物指出各组成部件的英文。

 Text 课文

 Power Steering System

During the traveling of the car, steering movement is the most basic movement. We manipulate and control the vehicle's rotating direction by using the steering wheel in order to realize our intentions. Automobile steering system can be divided into the manual steering system and the power steering system by different energy of steering. The manual steering system relies on the driver's steering power to steer the wheel.

Under the control of the driver, the power steering system can steer the wheel through the use of liquid pressure produced by the engine or motor driving force. As is shown in Figure 12-1, it is a hydraulic power steering system.

The electronic control power steering system (EPS, Figure 12-2) could make

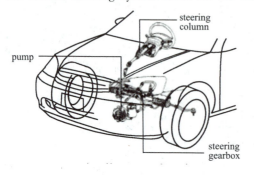

Figure 12-1 A hydraulic power steering system

steering wheel convenient and flexible at low speeds; steering in the region to high-speed, the EPS also promises to provide optimal power magnification and stability to handle, thus enhancing the stability of the control during high-speed traveling. So it has been commonly used in car manufacturing in every country.

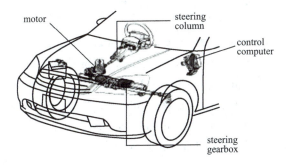

Figure 12 – 2   The electronic control power steering system

Power Steering System Service

The key components that make up a power steering system are the steering wheel, the steering column, the steering shaft, the steering gear, the pitman arm, the drag link, the pump, the rotary valve, the rack-and-pinion steering, the recirculating-ball steering (Figure 12 – 3).

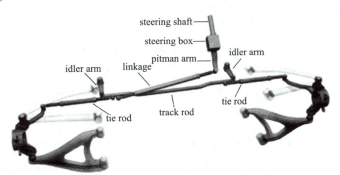

Figure 12 – 3   The recirculating-ball steering system

If these components could fail, they would require repair or replacement. The power steering system service typically consists of the following.

1. Checking the Power Steering Fluid

Basic procedures for checking the level of the power steering fluid are as follows.

(1) Turn off the engine of your car. With the parking brake set, place the transmission in either PARK or NEUTRAL.

Open the hood and find the reservoir for the power-steering fluid. It will probably be labeled on the cap. If not, look near the belts for a pulley-driven pump with a plastic or metal reservoir on top (Many cars today use a semi-transparent reservoir for power steering fluid).

(2) Unscrew and remove the cap to the power steering reservoir.

(3) Check the fluid level. If the reservoir is made of clear plastic, look for full and low indicator lines on the outside (Figure 12-4). The cap will have a small dipstick attached if the reservoir isn't see-through. Wipe the dipstick clean with a rag and put the cap back on. Remove the cap and check the level on the dipstick. Most dipsticks will have HOT and COLD markings.

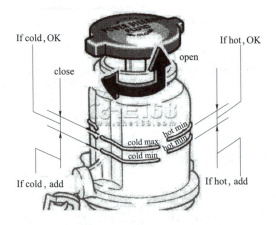

Figure 12-4 Clear plastic reservoir

 The fluid level will rise on the dipstick as the steering system warms.

If required, only add enough fluid to reach the correct mark on the dipstick. Automatic transmission fluid is commonly used in a power steering system. Some power steering systems, however, do NOT use automatic transmission fluid and require a special power steering fluid.

Always refer to the manufacturer's service for the correct type of fluid for your system.

2. Servicing the Power Steering Hoses and Belt

Always inspect the condition of the hoses and the belt very carefully. Hoses

Task 12 Power Steering System Services 99

typically deteriorate from the inside, which means they lose their effectiveness long before showing any external signs of deterioration or leaking. You'll know a hose has started to deteriorate if it feels soft and spongy. Oil and grease-soaked hoses should be replaced. Replace hard and brittle hoses because these will have lost their ability to expand and contract properly and then crack (Figure 12 – 5).

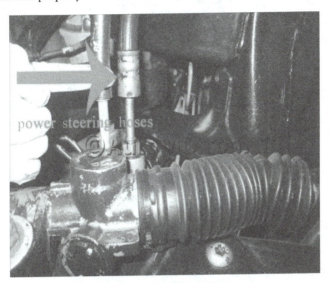

Figure 12 – 5 Power steering hoses

Look for exterior hose wear caused by abrasive contact with metal parts. This can eventually wear a hole in a hose and cause it to burst under pressure. Replace the hose and correct the reason for the damage. Reroute the hose and tighten the brackets using tie downs or rubber sheaths placed over the hose.

Note Power steering pump pressure can exceed 1,000 psi. This is enough to cause serious eye injury. Wear eye protection when working on a power steering system.

If it is necessary to replace a power steering hose, use a flare nut or tubing wrench. This action will prevent you from stripping the nut. When starting a new hose fitting, use your hand. This action will prevent cross threading. Always tighten the hose fitting properly.

A loose power steering belt (Figure 12 – 6 and Figure 12 – 7) can slip, decrease pump output and cause erratic operation. A worn or cracked belt may break during operation, which would cause a loss of power assist.

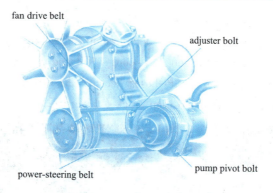

Figure 12 – 6 Power steering belt

Figure 12 – 7 Ease the belt onto the pulley

Note

When it is necessary to tighten a power steering belt, do NOT pry on the side of the power steering pump. The thin housing on the pump can easily be dented and ruined. ONLY pry on the reinforce flange or a recommended pry point.

The basic procedures for installing a power steering belt (Figure 12 – 8) are as follows.

(1) Loosen the bolts that hold the power steering pump to its brackets.

(2) Push inward on the pump to release tension on the belt. With the tension removed, slide the belt from the pulley.

(3) Obtain a new belt and install it in reverse order. Remember when adjusting belt tension to specifications, only pry on the reinforced flange or a recommended pry point.

Task 12 Power Steering System Services   101

Figure 12 – 8 Install a new belt

3. Power Steering Leaks

A common problem with power steering systems is fluid leakage. With pressure over 1,000 psi, typical leak points include the reservoir cap, the reservoir-to-pump-body seal, the shaft seal, the bolts, the fittings and the hose connections.

When checking for leaks, wipe the fluid-soaked area(s) with a clean rag. Then have another person start and idle the engine. While watching for leaks, have the steering wheel turned to the right and the left. This action will pressurize all components of the system that might be leaking. After locating the leaking component, repair or replace it.

A power steering pressure test (Figure 12 – 9) checks the operation of the power steering pump, the pressure relief valve, the control valve, the hoses, and the power piston. Basic procedures for performing a power steering pressure test are as follows.

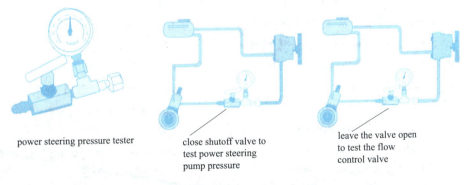

power steering pressure tester   close shutoff valve to test power steering pump pressure   leave the valve open to test the flow control valve

Figure 12 – 9 Test a power steering pressure

(1) Using a steering system pressure tester, connect the pressure gauge and shut off valve to the power steering pump outlet and hose. Torque the hose fitting properly.

(2) With the system full of fluid, start and idle the engine (with the shutoff valve open) while turning the steering wheel back and forth. This will bring the fluid up to

temperature.

(3) Close the shutoff valve to check system pressure. Note and compare the pressure reading with manufacturer's specifications.

Do NOT close the shutoff valve for more than 5 seconds. If the shutoff value is closed longer, damage will occur to the power steering pump from overheating.

4. Bleeding a Power Steering System

Any time you replace or repair a hydraulic component (pump, hoses, and power piston), you should bleed the system. Bleeding the system assures that all of the air is out of the hoses, the pump, and the gearbox. Air can cause the power steering system to make a BUZZING sound. The sound will occur as the steering wheel is turned right or left.

To bleed out any air, start the engine and turn the steering wheel fully from side to side. Keep checking the fluid and add as needed. This will force the air into the reservoir and out of the system.

New Words 生词

1. manipulate [mə'nipjuleit] v. (熟练地)操作,使用(机器等)
2. convenient [kən'vi:njənt] adj. 便利的,方便的
3. handle ['hændl] v. 处理,操作
4. hood [hud] n. 发动机罩
5. semi-transparent adj. 半透明的
6. unscrew ['ʌn'skru:] v. 从……旋出螺丝钉,旋松
7. dipstick ['dipstik] n. 量油计
8. deteriorate [di'tiəriəreit] v. (使)恶化
9. leaking ['li:kiŋ] n. 泄漏
10. spongy ['spʌndʒi] adj. 像海绵的,柔软的
11. burst [bə:st] v. 爆裂,爆发 n. 突然破裂
12. bracket ['brækit] n. 墙上凸出的托架,支架
13. sheath [ʃi:θ] n. 鞘,护套,外壳
14. wrench [rentʃ] n. 扳钳,扳手 v. 猛扭
15. strip [strip] v. 剥,剥去
16. reinforce [ˌri:in'fɔ:s] v. 加强,修补,加固
17. bolt [bəult] n. 门闩,螺钉
18. seal [si:l] n. 封铅,密封 v. 密封
19. pressurize ['preʃəraiz] v. 增压,密封,使……加压
20. hydraulic [hai'drɔ:lik] adj. 液压的,水压的
21. magnification [ˌmægnifi'keiʃən] n. 扩大,放大倍率

Task 12　Power Steering System Services

22. stability [stəˈbiliti] n. 稳定性
23. enhance [inˈhɑːns] v. 提高，增强
24. deterioration [diˌtiəriəˈreiʃən] n. 变坏，退化
25. reinforce [ˌriːinˈfɔːs] v. 加强，加固
26. bleed [bliːd] v. 泄（气，水）

Phrases and Expressions 短语与表达

1. steering column　　　　　转向管柱
2. steering shaft　　　　　　转向轴
3. pitman arm　　　　　　　转向摇臂
4. drag link　　　　　　　　直拉杆，转向纵拉杆
5. pressure relief valve　　　减压阀，安全阀
6. pressure gauge　　　　　压力计
7. rotary valve　　　　　　　回转阀，转阀；旋转阀
8. rack-and-pinion steering　齿条小齿轮转向机构
9. recirculating-ball　　　　　循环滚珠式的（转向机构）
10. metal reservoir　　　　　金属蓄水池
11. grease-soaked hose　　　浸油软管
12. shutoff valve　　　　　　截止阀，切断阀
13. pulley-driven pump　　　从动轮泵

Classroom Activities 课堂活动

Translate the English words in Figure 12-1 to Figure 12-3 into Chinese, and share with your classmates. (将图 12-1 ～ 图 12-3 中的英文单词翻译成中文，并与同学们分享。)

Grammar Notes 语法注释

Hoses typically deteriorate from the inside, which means they lose their effectiveness long before showing any external signs of deterioration or leaking.

其中 which 引导一个从句作主句的补充说明。"before showing any external signs of deterioration or leaking"是介词短语，做时间状语，意思是：在外部出现任何退化或泄漏迹象之前。

全句可译为：通常软管从内部开始恶化，这意味着在外部出现任何退化或泄漏迹象之前，软管很久以前就已经失去其效力。

◎ **Text Notes** 课文注释 ◎

1. The electronic control power steering system (EPS) could make steering wheel convenient and flexible at low speeds; steering in the region to high-speed, the EPS also promises to provide optimal power magnification and stability to handle, thus enhancing the stability of the control during high-speed traveling.

   电子控制动力转向系统(简称EPS),在低速行驶时可使转向轻便、灵活;当汽车在向高速区域转向的过程中,它又能保证提供最优的动力放大倍率和稳定的转向手感,从而提高了高速行驶的操纵稳定性。

2. A loose power steering belt can slip, decrease pump output and cause erratic operation.

   动力转向带松弛,就会产生滑动,将会减少泵的排量,并导致运转不稳定。

3. With pressure over 1,000 psi, typical leak points include the reservoir cap, the reservoir-to-pump-body seal, the shaft seal, the bolts, the fittings and the hose connections.

   如果压力大于1 000 psi (1 psi = 6.86 kPa),典型的泄漏点包括储液罐盖、储液罐到泵体的密封处、轴封、螺钉、接头以及软管连接处。

◎ **Safety Tips** 安全提示 ◎

(1) 请勿对转向系统的零部件进行热处理,否则可能产生的材料特性的变化将对车辆的安全运转有负面的影响。

(2) 在拆卸和安装转向系统(转向机、转向横拉杆、转向管柱等)时,转向机构必须在"直向前"位置。

(3) 只能使用认可的专用转向液,不要重复使用已排出的转向液。

◎ **Exercises** 练习

Part I Choose the best answers from the following choices according to the text.

1. The automobile steering system can _____ the manual steering system and the power steering system by different energies of steering.
   A. divide into   B. be divided from   C. be divided into   D. divide

2. _____ the parking brake set, place the transmission in either PARK or NEUTRAL.
   A. With   B. When   C. While   D. Although

3. If the reservoir _____ clear plastic, look for full and low indicator lines on the outside.
   A. is made of   B. is made for   C. make into   D. make out of

Task 12 Power Steering System Services

4. If required, only add enough fluid to reach the correct mark on the _____.
   A. reservoir   B. dipstick   C. indicator line   D. level
5. Someone always _____ the manufacturer's service for the correct type of fluid for your system.
   A. refers to   B. looks up   C. checks on   D. checks in
6. You'll know a hose has started to deteriorate _____ it feels soft and spongy.
   A. whether   B. if   C. that   D. when
7. This can _____ wear a hole in a hose and cause it to burst under pressure.
   A. definitively   B. finally   C. in the end   D. eventually
8. When it is necessary to _____ a power steering belt, do NOT pry on the side of the power steering pump.
   A. tighten   B. loosen   C. install   D. fix

Part II   Translate the following into Chinese.
1. pitman arm   2. pulley-driven pump
3. see-through   4. steering wheel
5. rubber sheath   6. prevent... from...
7. push on   8. in reverse order
9. back and forth   10. bleed out

Part III   Translate the following into English.
1. 回转阀   2. 浸油软管
3. 驻车   4. 擦去
5. 拴住   6. 扳手
7. 动力转向泵   8. 变速箱
9. 截止阀   10. 拉紧支架

Part IV   Translate the following sentences into Chinese.
1. We manipulate and control the vehicle's traveling direction by using the steering wheel, so as to realize our intentions.
2. If not, look near the belts for a pulley-driven pump with a plastic or metal reservoir on top (Many cars today use a semi-transparent reservoir for power steering fluid).
3. Hoses typically deteriorate from the inside, which means they lose their effectiveness long before showing any external signs of deterioration or leaking.
4. A worn or cracked belt may break during operation, which would cause a loss of power assist.
5. The basic procedures for installing a power steering belt are as follows:
   (1) Loosen the bolts that hold the power steering pump to its brackets.
   (2) Push inward on the pump to release tension on the belt. With the tension

removed, slide the belt from the pulley.

(3) Obtain a new belt and install it in reverse order. Remember when adjusting belt tension to specifications; only pry on the reinforced flange or a recommended pry point.

6. Using a steering system pressure tester, connect the pressure gauge and shutoff valve to the power steering pump outlet and hose.

7. With the system full of fluid, start and idle the engine (with the shutoff valve open) while turning the steering wheel back and forth.

Part V   Complete the questions based on the graphs below.

1. There is a couple of key components in the power steering graph in addition to the rack-and-pinion or recirculating-ball mechanism. Please indicate arrow parts.

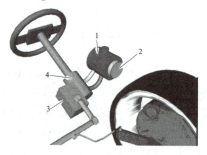

2. The hydraulic power for the steering is provided by a rotary-vane pump (See the diagram below). This pump is driven by the car's engine via a belt and pulley. Please make out the purpose of the pressure-relief valve.

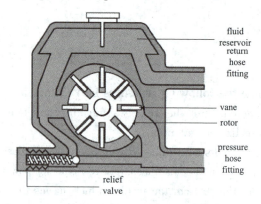

Task 13

Air Conditioning System Services
空调系统检测维修

学习目标:
1. 掌握空调系统的专业术语(英文);
2. 熟悉空调系统检测维修方法。

Text 课文

The A/C system has two major parts: The high side starts at the compressor and ends at the expansion device (orifice tube or expansion valve). The low side starts at the expansion device and ends at the compressor (Figure 13-1).

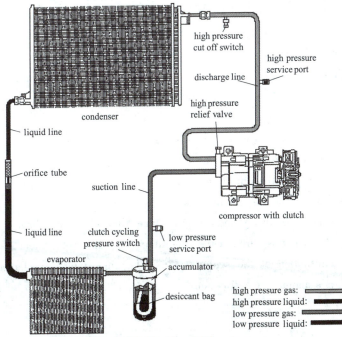

Figure 13-1 The A/C system

The pressure on the liquid R - 134a drops as it passes through the orifice tube. The low pressure allows it to boil and absorb heat in the evaporator. Heat transfers from the air passing through the evaporator to the liquid R - 134a. This heat boils the refrigerant, causing it to change state to a gas. The heat transfer cools the air.

1. Gauge Sets

Most service operations can be performed using a manifold and gauge set (Figure 13 -2). A gauge set has two gauges, two hand valves, and three service hoses.

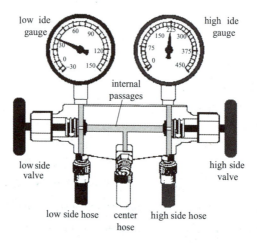

Figure 13 - 2　The manifold and gauge set

2. Service Units

Multiple service operations can be performed on the service units. Depending on the unit, they contain:

- A vacuum pump
- Refrigerant and a way of dispensing the proper amount
- A refrigerant recovery unit
- A refrigerant recycling unit
- Refrigerant oil dispensing unit

Service units require periodic maintenance. Recycling units have a filter that must be replaced when it is dirty. Other operations include replacement of the refrigerant tank, the calibration of the scale, and the vacuum pump oil changes. Check the manufacturer's maintenance directions.

Task 13 Air Conditioning System Services 109

3. A/C Service Procedures

1) Refrigerant Identification

The refrigerant in a system should be identified before recovery. Recovery of contaminated refrigerant can cause very expensive results. In our modern world, there are too many possibilities for contamination to take a chance. Identifiers sample the refrigerant in a system. Then they determine what it is composed of and print out or display the ingredients.

2) Sealant Detection

One source of contamination is from stop leaks/sealants. These can be put into a system and are designed to close refrigerant leaks. There are two general types: a seal conditioning type that causes O-rings and gaskets to swell and a sealant that is designed to close small holes. The second type hardens when it contacts moisture from air. Sealants can damage A/C service equipment. A quick detect sealant detector can be connected to a system to determine if the refrigerant contains sealant. Special service procedures are necessary if a sealant is detected.

3) Recovery Procedures

Most recovery units will shut off when the pressure drops to zero. Watch the pressure, if it rises after a few minutes, continue the recovery process. After recovery, check the amount of refrigerant and oil that were recovered.

Hint If you are recovering refrigerant from a system that has a leak, you will probably begin with a system that has low pressures. After this small amount of refrigerant has been recovered, there is a probability that the recovery unit will pull air through the leak. This air will be added to the refrigerant already recovered. Operate the recovery unit in a normal manner, but watch the operation. Recovery will probably take less time than normal. If the pressure drops to a low value yet does not continue to drop, the machine is probably pulling air from the outside. Stop the recovery.

4) Recycling

A recycle guard (special filter) can be connected into the hose entering the recovery machine. It will trap and filter out sealant, oil, and dye from the recovered refrigerant. The trapped materials should be drained out after each recovery. Note the cutaway portion to show one of the two filters(Figure 13 – 3).

The recycling operation depends on the service unit. The unit has a display screen to show the machine operations and a key pad for the technician to enter the job to be done.

5) Services by Using a Manifold and Gauge Set

The center hose of the manifold is connected to a vacuum pump during the evacuation process. It is connected to a refrigerant source while charging a system. Note that the manifold valves are open or closed as needed (Figure 13-4).

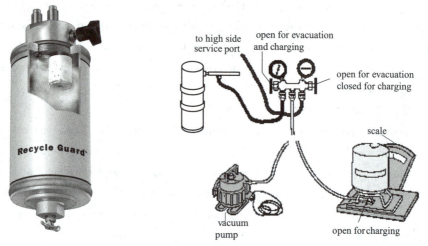

Figure 13-3　A recycle guard　　　Figure 13-4　Evacuation or charging using a manifold

6) Evacuation

(1) During evacuation using a manifold, the center hose is connected to the vacuum pump. Both hand valves are opened, and the pump is operated to pull all of the air and water out of a system. Air is removed with any other gas. If the pressure drops to 29.9 in.Hg, there will be no gas left in the system.

(2) Evacuation using a service unit (Figure 13-5) is essentially the same as using a manifold and vacuum pump.

Figure 13-5　Evacuation using a service unit

Water is removed from a system by dropping the pressure to cause it to boil. The boiling point of water at 29.2 in. Hg is 70 °F.

7) Vacuum Leak Check

When evacuation process reaches full vacuum, shut off both High and Low valves, and observe the vacuum reading. This vacuum should hold for several minutes. A leak in the system is indicated if the pressure rises.

8) Charging

This is the process of putting the correct amount of refrigerant into the system. A manifold (shown) or service unit can be used to charge. In this case, gas will be leaving the refrigerant container and entering the low side with the system running (Figure 13-6).

Charging from a large container while using a manifold requires a means to measure the refrigerant. A scale or a dial-a-charge (Figure 13-7) can be used. The scale can be programmed to shut after the correct charge has left the container. A service unit is programmed with the correct charge amount, and the process is begun. Refrigerant is then transferred from the machine to the system.

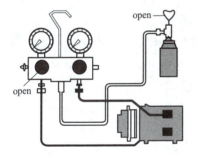

Figure 13-6 Charging by using a manifold

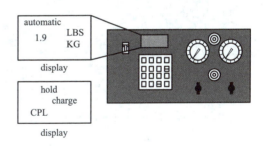

Figure 13-7 A dial-a-charge

9) Leak Detection and System Check

It is always a good practice to check any fittings that were disturbed to make sure there are no leaks. The system should be operated to make sure that the operating pressure is correct, the air discharge from the ducts is a cool temperature, and the compressor and drive belts are running properly and quietly.

New Words 生词

1. cutaway [ˈkʌtəwei] adj. 下摆圆角的，一部分切掉的
2. compressor [kəmˈpresə] n. 压缩机
3. evaporator [iˈvæpəreitə] n. 蒸发器，脱水器

4. manifold [ˈmænifəuld] n. 歧管
5. evacuation [iˌvækjuˈeiʃən] n. 排放,抽空
6. trap [træp] n. 收集,捕获
7. coupler [ˈkʌplə] n. 耦合器,联结器
8. flowmeter [ˈfləumiːtə] n. 流量计
9. refrigerant [riˈfridʒərənt] n. 制冷剂
10. recovery [riˈkʌvəri] n. 回收
11. recycle [ˈriːˈsaikl] v./n. 再循环

➡ Phrases and Expressions 短语与表达

1. vacuum pump	真空泵
2. cutaway portion	剖视图
3. O-ring	O形圈
4. manifold and gauge set	歧管量表装置
5. display screen	显示屏
6. key pad	键盘
7. stop leaks/sealants	防漏密封剂
8. dial-a-charge	数码灌装机
9. in. Hg	英寸汞柱(压力单位,1 in.Hg 相当于 25.4 mmHg)
10. relief valve	安全阀
11. orifice tube	节流管
12. clutch cycling pressure switch	(空调)压力离合器循环开关
13. R-134a	环保型空调制冷剂
14. service port	检测接口
15. accumulator	储液器
16. desiccant bag	干燥剂包
17. suction line	抽吸管
18. high pressure cut off switch	高压切断开关
19. recycle guard	循环装置

🔹 Classroom Activities 课堂活动

Translate the English words in Figure 13-1, Figure 13-2 into Chinese; share these words with your classmates. (将图 13-1、图 13-2 的英文单词翻译成中文,并与同学们分享。)

Task 13　Air Conditioning System Services

◎ Grammar Notes 语法注释 ◎

Evacuation using a service unit is essentially the same as using a manifold and vacuum pump.

句子中的"using a service unit"是一个现在分词短语,用来修饰限定"Evacuation"。"using a manifold and vacuum pump"的作用也是一样。

全句可译为:用维修设备排放和用歧管量表及真空泵排放,其效果是完全一样的。

◎ Text Notes 课文注释 ◎

1. The A/C system has two major parts: The high side starts at the compressor and ends at the expansion device. The low side starts at the expansion device and ends at the compressor.
   空调系统可以分为两大部分:高压侧始于压缩机,结束于膨胀阀;低压侧始于膨胀阀,结束于压缩机。

2. Most recovery units will shut off when the pressure drops to zero.
   大多数回收系统在压力降到零时都会自动关闭。

3. Note that the manifold valves are open or closed as needed.
   要注意的是,歧管量表装置的阀门的开闭视具体情况而定。

4. In our modern world, there are too many possibilities for contamination to take a chance.
   在当今世界,可能发生的污染有很多,因此我们不能掉以轻心。

5. Charging from a large container while using a manifold requires a means to measure the refrigerant.
   当用歧管量表装置从大容器向空调系统加注制冷剂时,得有一个计量制冷剂的办法。

6. The system should be operated to make sure that the operating pressure is correct, the air discharge from the ducts is a cool temperature, and the compressor and drive belts are running properly and quietly.
   应起动空调系统,检查压力是否正常,看放出的空气凉不凉,压缩机和传动带运转是否平稳、安静。

◎ Safety Tips 安全提示 ◎

(1) 在加注时,应戴好防护手套,以免制冷剂滴到皮肤上冻伤皮肤。
(2) 空调的制冷剂不能直接排放到大气中,报废的制冷剂必须加以回收。
(3) 空调系统机油含有被溶解的制冷剂,属于危险废弃物,必须送到指定地点进行处理或回收。

Exercises 练习

Part I Choose the best answers from the following choices according to the text.

1. The pressure on the liquid R – 134a drops as it passes through the _____.
   A. compressor   B. orifice tube
   C. recovery   D. gauge set

2. Recycling units have a filter _____ must be replaced when it is dirty.
   A. it   B. who   C. them   D. that

3. The refrigerant in a system should be _____ before recovery.
   A. cool   B. changed   C. identified D. print out

4. The _____ of the manifold is connected to a vacuum pump during the evacuation process.
   A. center hose   B. low side hose
   C. high side hose   D. valve

5. During evacuation using a manifold, the center hose is connected to the vacuum pump. _____ are opened.
   A. Both hand valves   B. Low side hoses
   C. Orifice tubes   D. Low side valves

6. The system should be operated to _____ the operating pressure is correct.
   A. do   B. make   C. cause   D. make sure that

7. _____ service operations can be performed by using a manifold and gauge set.
   A. Each   B. A little   C. Few   D. Most

8. Most recovery units will _____ when the pressure drops to zero.
   A. open   B. shut off   C. take off   D. drop

9. The A/C system has two major parts: The high side starts at the _____ and ends at the expansion device.
   A. compressor   B. condenser   C. orifice tube   D. vacuum pump

10. A gauge set has _____ gauges, two hand valves, and three service hoses.
    A. one   B. three   C. two   D. four

Part II Translate the following into English.

1. 压缩机   2. 制冷剂
3. 蒸发器   4. 节流管
5. 真空泵   6. 泄漏
7. 冷凝器   8. 吸热
9. 定期维修   10. 密封剂

Task 13 Air Conditioning System Services

Part III Translate the following into Chinese.

1. compress
2. vacuum pump
3. dial-a-charge
4. accumulator
5. recycle guard
6. evacuation
7. filter out
8. manifold and gauge set
9. display screen
10. service port
11. relief valve
12. sealant

Part IV Translate the following sentences into Chinese.

1. When evacuation process reaches full vacuum, shut off both High and Low valves, and observe the vacuum reading. This vacuum should hold for several minutes. A leak in the system is indicated if the pressure rises.
2. The A/C system has two major parts: The high side starts at the compressor and ends at the expansion device (orifice tube or expansion valve). The low side starts at the expansion device and ends at the compressor.
3. The pressure on the liquid R-134a drops as it passes through the orifice tube.
4. Most service operations can be performed by using a manifold and gauge set. A gauge set has two gauges, two hand valves, and three service hoses.
5. Charging from a large container while using a manifold and gauge set requires a means to measure the refrigerant.
6. Evacuation using a service unit is essentially the same as using a manifold and vacuum pump.
7. Water is removed from a system by dropping the pressure to cause it to boil. The boiling point of water at 29.2 in.Hg is 70 °F.
8. The center hose of the manifold and gauge set is connected to a vacuum pump during the evacuation process.

Part V Complete the questions based on the chart given below.

1. In this TXV system(膨胀阀空调系统), place an H where the high side begins and an L where the low side begins.

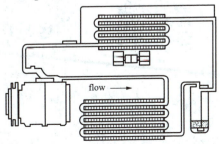

2. Place an L on the liquid flow tube side and a G on the gas flow tube side.

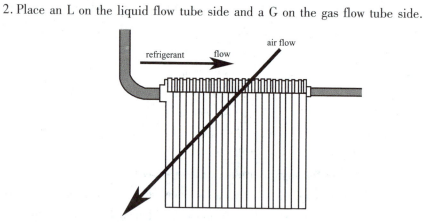

3. Which service is shown in this chart?

译文答案

发音训练

Task 14

Lighting System Service Manual
照明系统维修手册

学习目标：
1. 掌握照明系统的专业英文词汇；
2. 能借助英文理解丰田汉兰达车型照明系统的英文维修手册。

 Text 课文

 Lighting System

The automotive lamp assembly is the basic component of the group lighting, which comprises three parts: light (bulb), the mirror reflector and light transmittance.

Automotive lamps with different functions can be divided into two categories: lighting and signal lamps (Figure 14-1 and Figure 14-2). Lighting includes: the headlamp (low beams and high beams), the fore-fog-lamp, the reversing light and the side marker light. Signal lights include: the location light, the turn signal, the brake light, the rear-fog-lamp, the license plate lamp and the retroreflector.

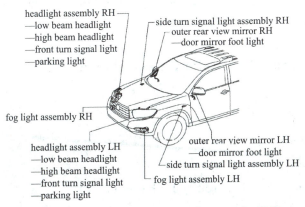

Figure 14-1 The parts location of automotive lights

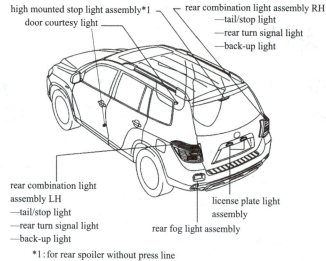

Figure 14 – 2　The parts location of automotive signal lights

1. Headlight

The headlight, loaded with different light sources, can be divided into the gas light (gas discharge light) and the electric light (filament light). There are also incandescent lights and halogen tungsten lights. In order to further improve the safety of automobile driving, LED technology is applied to the design of automobile lamps by the designers.

2. Fog Lamps

The fog lamp is mainly used in condition of fog, snow, rain or dust. To prevent oncoming vehicle drivers' dazzling, the projection distance of fog lamps beam is nearer on the ground relative to the low beam.

Toyota Highlander Repair Manual

1. Headlight

Disassembly

(1) Remove the headlight cover.

(2) Remove No. 1 headlight bulb (Figure 14 – 3).

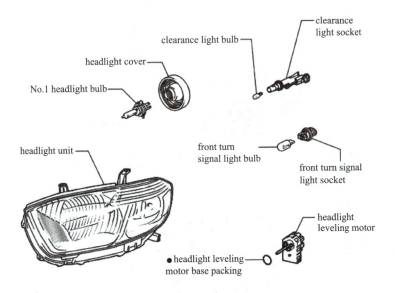

Figure 14 – 3 A headlight unit

(3) Remove front turn signal light bulb.
(4) Remove clearance light bulb.
(5) Remove headlight leveling motor.
(6) Remove headlight leveling motor base packing.

Notice:

After the headlight leveling motor base packing is removed, be sure to replace it with a new one. Failure to do this may cause water ingress.

When headlights are replaced or any time front-end work is performed on the vehicle, the headlights should be aimed using the proper equipment. Headlights not properly aimed can make it virtually impossible to see and may blind other drivers on the road, causing injury or death.

Reassembly

(1) Install headlight leveling motor base packing.
(2) Install headlight leveling motor.
(3) Install clearance light bulb.
(4) Install front turn signal light bulb.
(5) Install No. 1 headlight bulb.
(6) Install headlight cover.

2. Fog light

Disassembly

(1) Remove cool air intake duct seal (Figure 14 – 4).
(2) Remove radiator grille.

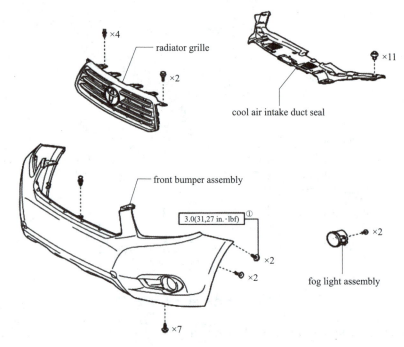

Figure 14-4　The components of fog light assembly

(3) Remove front bumper assembly.

(4) Remove fog light assembly.

(5) Remove fog light bulb.

Notice:

Do not touch the bulb glass.

Reassembly

(1) Install fog light bulb.

(2) Install fog light assembly.

(3) Install front bumper assembly.

(4) Install radiator grille.

(5) Install cool air intake duct seal.

(6) Preparation for fog light aiming.

(7) Inspect fog light aiming.

(8) Adjust fog light aiming.

---

① 1 in.·lbf = 0.113 N·m。

Task 14　Lighting System Service Manual

New Words 生词

1. comprise [kəmˈpraiz] v. 组成,构成,包括,包含
2. category [ˈkætigəri] n. 种类,类别
3. headlight [ˈhedlait] n. 前照灯
4. retroreflector [ˈretrəuriˈflektə(r)] n. 回射器,后向反射器
5. disassembly [ˌdisəˈsembəli] n. 拆卸
6. reassembly [riˈəsembli] n. 重新组合,重新组装
7. oncoming [ˈɔnkʌmiŋ] adj. 即将来临的 n. 来临
8. combination [kambiˈneiʃ(ə)n] n. 结合,联合,混合,组合
9. rear [riə(r)] adj. 后面的,后部的
10. distance [ˈdistəns] n. 距离,远处,间距
11. remove [riˈmu:v] v. 去除,去掉,移开,拆卸
12. assembly [əˈsembli] n. 集会;总成

➡ Phrases and Expressions 短语与表达

1. light transmittance　　　透光度
2. low beam　　　近光束,近光灯
3. high beam　　　远光束,远光灯
4. reversing light　　　倒车灯
5. back-up light　　　倒车灯
6. side marker light　　　侧灯
7. location light　　　定位灯,方位灯
8. turn signal light　　　转向信号灯
9. brake light　　　制动灯
10. license plate lamp　　　牌照灯
11. gas discharge light　　　气体放电灯
12. filament light (incandescent light)　　　白炽灯
13. tungsten light　　　钨丝灯
14. fog light　　　雾灯
15. in order to…　　　为了……
16. in condition of…　　　在……条件下
17. clearance light bulb　　　插口式灯泡

18. tail light	尾灯
19. door courtesy light	门控灯
20. radiator grille	散热器护栏
21. front bumper	前保险杠
22. high-mounted stop light	高位制动灯
23. bulb socket	灯泡座
24. cool air intake duct seal	冷风进气管密封件

Classroom Activities 课堂活动

1. Flashcard identification: Let the students try to match the English flashcards with the Chinese ones. (卡片识别:让同学们尝试英文卡片与中文卡片的匹配。活动方法:以小组为学习单位,小组成员之间进行中、英文卡片的匹配;选出两组代表进行比赛。)

    Flashcards(卡片):headlamp 前照灯,high beam 远光灯,low beam 近光灯,fog light 雾灯,brake light 制动灯,turn signal light 转向灯,location light 方位灯,backup light 倒车灯,license plate lamp 牌照灯,bulb socket 灯泡座。

2. scrambled words quiz game(单词重组游戏):应用交互式电子白板互动课堂工具,设计单词学习游戏,让学生进行单词游戏训练(老师可复制、更换单词)。在训练模板上输入5个单词,通过移动小球顺序而获得正确单词的游戏方式(计时)来完成这一组单词的重组训练。学生可在老师及同伴的协助下参与训练,以增强课堂中的师生互动、生生互动。

    (游戏操作方法及截屏说明放在信息化教学教案里;动态的游戏课件与教案一起放在信息化教学资源文件夹里。)

Text Notes 课文注释

1. In order to further improve the safety of automobile driving, LED technology is applied to the design of automobile lamps by the designers.
   为了进一步提升汽车的驾驶安全性,设计者将LED技术应用到汽车灯具设计之中。

2. The fog lamp is used mainly in condition of fog, snow, rain or dust.
   雾灯主要用于雾、雪、雨或者灰尘的天气情况下。

3. After the headlight leveling motor base packing is removed, be sure to replace it with a new one. Failure to do this may cause water ingress.

Task 14 Lighting System Service Manual

拆卸前照灯调平电动机底座填料后,确保更换一个新的,否则可能会导致有水浸入。

4. Preparation for fog light aiming.

   做好雾灯校准的准备。

Safety Tips 安全提示

(1) 卤素灯泡内含有压力气体,如果过热会发生爆炸。不要用手摸卤素灯泡的玻璃部分。在卤素灯泡处进行检修或维护操作时,要佩戴防护眼镜。
(2) 驾车时不要为了能看到很远的地方,一直使用远光灯。
(3) 不要到变更车道时或快要转弯时才打开转向灯。
(4) 左转时要注意后方来车。
(5) 错过转弯处时不要强行变更车道。
(6) 雨中开车要将前照灯打开,最好把防雾灯也打开。

Exercises 练习

Part I Choose the best answers from the following choices according to the text.

1. The automotive lamp assembly is the basic component of the group lighting, which comprises three parts: the light bulb, the mirror reflector and the _____.
   A. ceiling lamp   B. fog lamp
   C. light transmittance   D. brake light

2. Some headlights have a single bulb with two _____, one for high beam and the other for low beam.
   A. filaments   B. turn signals   C. location lights   D. filament lights

3. Automotive lights with different functions can be divided into two categories: lighting and _____.
   A. signal lights   B. dash lamps   C. brake lights   D. tungsten lamps

4. _____ is directed so that it illuminates the road straight ahead of the vehicle.
   A. Headlight   B. Low beam   C. Fog light   D. High beam

5. The _____ is directed lower and to the left side so that it is away from oncoming vehicles.
   A. Headlight   B. Low beam   C. Fog light   D. High beam

6. _____ are used to reflect the light beams from the reflector.
   A. Patterned lenses   B. Headlights
   C. Brake lights   D. Fog lights

7. Headlights can be divided into _____ and electric lights (filament lights).

   A. bulb sockets　　B. reversing lights　　C. gas lights　　D. dash lights

8. Apart from shape and size, headlight lenses can be either patterned or _____.

   A. open　　B. clear　　C. closed　　D. moist

9. The _____ is used to protect the bulb and the reflector.

   A. lens　　B. bulb filament　　C. headlights　　D. high beam

10. The _____ is positioned in relation to the reflector so that the correct focus is obtained.

    A. lens　　B. high beam　　C. headlight　　D. bulb filament

Part II　Translate the following into English.

1. 侧灯
2. 前照灯
3. 灯泡座
4. 高位制动灯
5. 定位灯
6. 透光度
7. 倒车灯
8. 牌照灯
9. 近光灯
10. 雾灯

Part III　Translate the following into Chinese.

1. door courtesy light
2. tail light
3. brake light
4. turn signal light
5. high beam
6. filament light
7. bulb socket
8. radiator grille
9. tungsten light
10. gas discharge light

Part IV　Translate the following sentences into Chinese.

1. The headlight, loaded with different light sources, can be divided into the gas light (gas discharge light) and the electric light (filament light).

2. Signal lights include: the location light, the turn signal, the brake light, the rear-fog-lamp, the license plate light and the retroreflector.

3. To prevent oncoming vehicle drivers' dazzling, the projection distance of fog lamps beam is nearer on the ground relative to the low beam.

4. Headlights not properly aimed can make it virtually impossible to see and may blind other drivers on the road, causing injury or death.

Part V　Complete the questions based on the graphs below.

1. What is the difference between these two types of bulbs in the figure below?

Task 14 Lighting System Service Manual

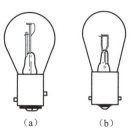

(a)　　(b)

2. Point out the parts of a headlamp assembly with a quartz halogen bulb in the figure below.

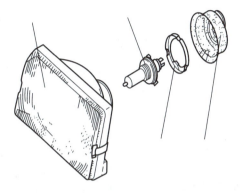

3. Look at the figure below and label the parts correctly.

Part II

Automobile Marketing and Services

汽车营销与服务篇

Task 15

Automobile Trading
汽车交易

学习目标:
1. 掌握汽车商务礼仪及促销的专业英文术语;
2. 了解广州交易会的盛况;
3. 熟悉参观4S店对话的专业用语。

 Text 课文

 15.1 Business Courtesy for Vehicle

There is a popular Chinese saying "Nothing could be happier than having friends coming afar." It is a traditional way to show our courtesy and our hospitality in business activities. We will start by meeting business partners at the airport, at the booth of exhibition, at the dinner party, at the hotel or at any other public places, as well as communicating by telephone, and all the way up to a contract concluded at end. We wish to treat our business partners as good friends. At any business activity, the host is to greet and introduce himself, or exchange the name card at first. It shows a good beginning of the coming negotiation, and provides a chance for both parties to get to know each other further.

 15.2 Promotion

Promotion is to present the product to the potential customers. It involves the presentation of the product, the brand name and image, the packing, the advertising, the literature, the catalogue, the price list, the after-sale service, the training, the trade fair and exhibition, the public relations as well as personal selling and so on.

Promoting stands for activities that communicate the features and advantages of the product directly, then persuade potential customers to purchase it. Promoting any product includes using a "Feature Advantage Benefit (FAB)." There are four effects in the FAB promotion work rule.

(1) To attract the attention of potential customers.

(2) To create interest of potential customers.

(3) To arouse a desire for its benefit.

(4) To encourage the customers to take prompt action.

New Words 生词

1. negotiation [niˌgəuʃi'eiʃən] n. 谈判;转让
2. consultation [ˌkɔnsəl'teiʃən] n. 咨询;磋商;讨论会
3. import [im'pɔːt 'impɔːt] n. 进口,进口货 v. 进口
4. export [ik'spɔːt, 'ekspɔːt] n. 输出,出口;出口商品 v. 出口
5. promise ['prɔmis] n. 许诺;希望 v. 允诺,许诺
6. interdependent [ˌintədi'pendənt] adj. 相互依赖的;互助的
7. interaction [ˌintər'ækʃn] n. 相互作用;交互作用
8. assessment [ə'sesmənt] n. 评定;估价
9. participant [pɑː'tisipənt] adj. 参与的 n. 参与者
10. agenda [ə'dʒendə] n. 议程
11. courtesy ['kəːtisi] n. 礼貌 adj. 出于礼节的
12. booth [buːð, buːθ] n. 展位;货摊;公用电话亭
13. promotion [prəu'məuʃən] n. 提升;推销,促销
14. potential [pəu'tenʃəl] n. 潜能 adj. 潜在的;可能的
15. customer ['kʌstəmə] n. 顾客
16. catalogue ['kætəlɔg] n. 目录 v. 把……编入目录
17. trade fair 商品交易会;贸易展销会
18. persuade [pə'sweid] v. 说服,劝说
19. purchase ['pəːtʃəs] n. 购买 v. 购买;赢得
20. arouse [ə'rauz] v. 引起;唤醒;鼓励;激发
21. benefit ['benifit] n. 利益,好处;救济金 v. 有益于
22. encourage [in'kʌridʒ] v. 鼓励,怂恿;激励;支持

Task 15　Automobile Trading

➡ Phrases and Expressions 短语与表达

1. as well as 　　　　　　　　　　　　又,也,以及
2. be based on 　　　　　　　　　　　基于……之上,建立在……基础上
3. all the way up to 　　　　　　　　直到,直至
4. Feature Advantage Benefit(FAB)work rule　FAB 陈述法

● Text Notes 课文注释

1. negotiation（n.）（动词为 negotiate）在信用证用语中的意思是"议付,承兑(票证)"。在商务用语中意为"谈判,商议"。
   e.g.（1）We presented a clean on board bill of lading for the negotiation of payment.
   　　　　议付时我们呈递了一份清洁装运提单。
   　　（2）The contract was the result of a long negotiation.
   　　　　合同的签订是长期谈判的结果。
2. catalogue　n. 产品目录,样本。
   a copy of catalogue of（product）一份某产品的目录。
   e.g. We are now enclosing a copy of catalogue of our chemical products.
   　　　我们现随函附上我方化学产品的目录一份。
   同义词语:catalogue——产品目录
   　　　　　pamphlet, booklet, brochure ——产品小册子
   　　　　　leaflet——单张说明书,广告单
   　　　　　literature——商品文字宣传资料的统称
3. purchase　v./n. 购买,购买的货物。
   Right now we are interested in the purchase of vehicles from China.
   现在我们有兴趣从中国购买车辆。
   同义词语:purchase, buy
   purchase 用于正式的或规模较大的商务活动,buy 为日常用语,商务中用得较少。
4. FAB 陈述法。
   通常向顾客介绍产品时,采用 FAB 陈述法陈述其产品的特点、优势以及利益等方面的问题。FAB 是英文单词 feature, advantage, benefit 的缩写。

15.3　Automobile Fairs

　　The Chinese Import & Export Commodities Fair is held twice every year in the city of Guangzhou. The spring session of the fair lasts from April 15 to May 5 and the autumn session of the fair lasts from October 15 to November 5. Tens of thousands of international businessmen come to the fair from all over the world. Foreign businessmen are attracted by the various kinds of products on display at the fair, and they feel that

Chinese export products are of good quality and reasonable in price. At the fair, foreign businessmen have negotiations with Chinese exporters, and a lot of contracts are signed.

Wuhan Dazhong Automobile Manufacture Co., Ltd. has attended the spring session of the Guangzhou Fair. Mr. Anderson Green, America Ocean Trade Corporation has visited the booth of Wuhan Dazhong Automobile Manufacture Co., Ltd. on display.

The following is a business communication between Mr. Anderson Green and Miss Zhang Hailing.

Zhang: Good morning! You are welcome to our booth and look around our new cars—Citroën C5 series. My name is Zhang Hailing, electronic engineer from Wuhan Dazhong Automobile Manufacture Co., Ltd. Here is my name card.

Green: Good morning, Miss Zhang Hailing, nice to meet you. I have the pleasure to take this opportunity to visit your products. I am Anderson Green coming from the U.S.A. Here is my business card.

Zhang: Well, from your business card, I know that you are sales manager specializing in vehicles.

Green: That's right. I have been in this line for about 10 years. Our vehicles are exported to many countries. I am also interested in your products; I anticipate that the prospects for your Citroën C5 series especially for central American market promise very well.

Zhang: Yes. This series has been exported to various European countries. I hope to have a chance of cooperation with you at this time.

Green: All right. I think so. Could you please give some information about this series?

Zhang: Of course. You're also welcome to enquire anything about this series.

Green: It would be appreciated if you would give me a profile of this new car.

Zhang: All right. From its bright exterior lines to its beautiful interior, our new car Citroën C5 series performs with style, whether you're cruising a scenic beach highway or driving out in the countryside. The standard full-way power driver seat and available melodious sound system help to make your travel special. So does the standard cruise control. Your requirements and needs will be both met with Citroën C5 series. Besides AM/FM stereo with cassette/CD players, radio data system (RDS), seek and scan, digital clock, automatic tone control, speed compensated volume and theft lock as well as power tilt-sliding sunroof, it also includes inside rearview electro chronic mirror and outside rearview blue-tint mirror.

Green: It's simply wonderful. Go ahead please.

Task 15 Automobile Trading

Zhang: Here I would like to give a briefing of 2 different types of this series product at your option. This is Citroën C5 – 2.0 L. It has many features such as safety, comfort, convenience and so forth. The specification is as follows: engine 2.0 liters L4, 147 hp, transmission 4 way manual/automatic, max. speed 200 km/per hour, oil consumption 9.4. The other type is Citroën C5 – 3.0 L. It is a luxurious type with engine 3.0 liters V6, 220 hp, transmission 6 way manual/automatic, max. speed 230/per hour, oil consumption 10.5.

Green: Good! I am very keen on your introduction.

Zhang: Should you have further question, please do not hesitate to contact me at any time. You're also welcome to visit the head office of our company in Wuhan.

Green: I am sure. Thank you.

New Words 生词

1. commodity [kəˈmɔditi] n. 商品,货物;日用品
2. fair [fɛə] adj. 公平的 adv. 公平地 n. 展览会;交易会
3. contract v. [kənˈtrækt] 收缩;订约 n. [ˈkɔntrækt] 合同
4. display [disˈplei] n. 显示;炫耀 v. 显示;表现;陈列
5. anticipate [ænˈtisipeit] v. 预期,期望;占先,抢先;提前使用
6. prospect [ˈprɔspekt] n. 前途;预期
7. cooperation [kəuˌɔpəˈreiʃən] n. 合作,协作;协力
8. appreciate [əˈpriːʃieit] v. 欣赏;感激;领会
9. profile [ˈprəufail] n. 侧面;轮廓;简介
10. exterior [ikˈstiəriə] adj. 外部的 n. 外部
11. interior [inˈtiəriə] n. 内部;本质 adj. 内部的;国内的
12. style [stail] n. 风格;时尚;类型
13. cruise [kruːz] v. 巡航,巡游 n. 巡航
14. melodious [miˈləudjəs] adj. 悦耳的;旋律优美的
15. besides [biˈsaidz] adv. 此外;而且 prep. 除……之外
16. sunroof [ˈsʌnruːf] n. 汽车顶上可开启的遮阳篷顶
17. chronic [ˈkrɔnik] adj. 慢性的;长期的;习惯性的
18. exhaust [igˈzɔːst] v. 排出 n. 排气;废气;排气装置
19. consumption [kənˈsʌmpʃən] n. 消费;消耗;肺痨
20. hesitate [ˈheziteit] v. 犹豫 v. 踌躇,犹豫

➡ Phrases and Expressions 短语与表达

1. Chinese Import & Export Commodities Fair   中国进出口商品交易会
2. the spring session of the fair   春季交易会
3. the autumn session of the fair   秋季交易会
4. look round   游览,察看
5. specialize in   专门从事于
6. be interested in   对……感兴趣
7. full-way power driver seat   全方位动力驱动座椅
8. standard cruise control   标准的导航控制
9. AM/FM stereo with cassette/CD players   带CD立体声调幅/调频立体声播放机
10. seek and scan   自动扫描系统
11. power tilt-sliding sunroof   自动倾斜滑动天窗
12. rearview mirror   后视镜
13. 4 way manual/automatic   4挡手自一体

◆ Text Notes 课文注释

1. display   *n.* 陈列,展览。

   For your information, most of our vehicles will be on display at the Chinese Commodities Exhibition to be held in Wuhan soon.

   供贵方参考,不久在武汉举办的中国商品展览会上将展出我方大多数车辆产品。

   同义词语:display, show, exhibition。

2. anticipate   *v.* 期待,盼望。

   该词可接动名词,可接 that 从句,其过去分词可用作定语。

   (1) We anticipate having your early reply. 盼早日回复。
   (2) We anticipate that the goods will arrive next week.
       我们预计货物将于下周到达。
   (3) We thank you in advance for the anticipated favor.
       盼早日回复,并预致谢忱。

   同义词语:expect, look forward to。

   其中 expect 使用广泛,既可表示期待好的事物,也表示预料发生不喜爱的事情。

   anticipate 和 look forward to 表示怀着热切的心情而期盼,盼望喜闻乐见的事情。

3. Should you have further question, please do not hesitate to contact me at any time.

Task 15　Automobile Trading 135

如果您还有什么问题,请不必客气(不必犹豫),任何时间都可跟我联系。

该句为虚拟语气条件从句。把 should 提到句首,则将 if 省去,成为倒装句。主句中 hesitate 后多接动词不定式,也可接 about, over 等,后加名词或动名词,如:We are still hesitating about accepting the invitation to the party.

对是否接受参加聚会的邀请,我们仍在犹豫。

4. help to do sth. 对做……有帮助、有作用。课文中"So does the standard cruise control"为倒装句,so 放在句首,句子成为部分倒装。所谓部分倒装就是句子的谓语动词放在主语之前。

15.4　Visiting a 4S Shop

　　Mr. Zhang Xuan, executive president of Wuhan Dazhong Automobile Manufacture Co., Ltd. and Miss Dai Wei, an interpreter are waiting at the airport for the arrival of Miss Yanglin Zhang (Sugar), deputy managing director of America Ocean Trade Corporation from Boston.

Dai Wei： Excuse me, but aren't you Miss Yanglin Zhang? I am Dai Wei, an interpreter from Wuhan Dazhong Automobile Manufacture Co., Ltd.

Sugar： Yes. I am Yanglin Zhang from America Ocean Trade Corporation. How do you do? Here is my name card. Please call my English name Sugar.

Dai Wei： Good morning, Miss Sugar. May I introduce you to our executive president Mr. Zhang Xuan?

Zhang Xuan： Welcome to Wuhan, Miss Sugar. How do you do?

Sugar： Nice to meet you. It is very kind of you to come and meet me at the airport, dear Mr. Zhang Xuan.

Zhang Xuan： You're welcome. We're meeting you to visit the head office of our company and look around our 4S shop. This is a reception agenda.

Sugar： Oh! That is very thoughtful!

Dai Wei： Let's go, this way please.

Zhang Xuan： Miss Sugar, is this your first trip to Wuhan? How was the flight?

Sugar： Ah, pretty good; you know Wuhan is my home town. After I graduated from Huazhong University of Science and Technology, I went to Harvard University, the U.S.A. to go further my study for a doctor's degree, and now I am working for America Ocean Trade Corporation. I am deputy managing director of the corporation in charge of marketing.

Dai Wei:	Congratulations! You're deserved. Here we are now. Firstly, you have to stay in the room for a good rest, then we're together to lunch, we'll visit our 4S shop this afternoon, all right?
Sugar:	I think, time is urgent right now, so we'd like to visit your 4S shop instead.
Dai Wei:	That's OK.

A party of visitors, Miss Sugar, Miss Dai Wei and other persons arrived at the 4s shop.

Dai Wei:	Let's go through into the show room please.
Sales man:	Thanks for your coming to our 4S shop, and offering excellent products and services is our duty. Please look around our products firstly. OK! This is the ideal product — Citroën C5 series. It has a good market this year.
Sugar:	Very good!
Sales man:	Here I would like to give a briefing of this series product at your option. From type Citroën C5 – 2.0 L, Citroën C5 – 3.0 L to Citroën C5 – 4.0 L, they're provided for family and business users, and they have many features such as safety, comfort, convenience and so forth. Besides, they also have some other advantages; their features are up-to-date; their price is reasonable; replacement of spare parts is convenient, and we can offer an excellent after-sale service promptly and reliably.
Sugar:	That's wonderful. Go ahead please.
Sales man:	Here are a series of catalogues for this new type, and I can answer any technical question about our products.
Sugar:	OK. Let me see your catalogues. I think this type will be well saleable in central America. Here is a list of my requirements for which I would like to have your lowest CIF Miami.
Sales man:	Thanks for your enquiry. Would you please give me the quantity you required so as to offer for you?
Sugar:	Of course. We shall be able to place substantial orders from you. Let me know your price lists.
Sales man:	OK! Here are our price lists. All the prices in the lists are subject to our final confirmation.
Sugar:	What about discount for these prices?
Sales man:	If your order is large, we're prepared to grant you a discount of 5% on the price.

Task 15 Automobile Trading

Sugar: That's all right. Although this is my first trip to visit your 4s shop, yet I have heard quite a lot about your company from our sales manager Mr. Green. He has been to the Spring Fair one month ago, and we have received your offer. After perusal of the terms and conditions of your quotation, we have found them acceptable, but only one question is that your price is too high for us to accept. You know that our order is for a much larger quantities.

Sales man: May I ask what is your idea of a much larger quantities?

Sugar: Approximately 100 units for a quarter.

Sales man: In order to conclude business with you, as a token of friendship, we're prepared to make a reduction of 6% on our quotation if your order is exactly larger enough.

Sugar: Much to our delight, we have brought this transaction to a successful conclusion.

Sales man: Thank you, we'll be waiting for your final confirmation.

Dai Wei: I appreciate our efforts and cooperation and hope that this will be the model of other business in the future.

Sugar: I think so. Although this is my first trip to visit your 4s shop, I have enjoyed this trip very much. It has really deepened my understanding of your company.

Dai Wei: I'm glad you found it worthwhile. Thank you very much for your coming.

New Words 生词

1. interpreter [in'tə:pritə] n. 解释者;口译者
2. prospect ['prɔspekt] n. 前途;预期
3. subsidiary [səb'sidiəri] adj. 附属的;辅助的 n. 子公司;辅助者
4. marketing ['ma:kitiŋ] n. 行销,销售 v. 出售
5. instead [in'sted] adv. 代替;反而
6. discount ['diskaunt] n. 折扣;贴现率 v. 打折扣
7. perusal [pə'ru:zəl] n. 熟读;精读;细读;审核
8. worthwhile ['wə:θ'hwail] adj. 值得做的,值得花时间的

➡ Phrases and Expressions 短语与表达

1. deputy managing director   董事副总经理
2. executive president   常务总经理,执行总经理,副总经理
3. open up   开辟,开拓
4. look back   回顾
5. welding machine   电焊机
6. automobile charger   汽车充电器
7. in charge of   从事,负责
8. to be deserved   值得,称得起,配得上
9. too... to   太……以致不能
10. as a token of   作为……的象征(标志)

⬤ Text Notes 课文注释 ⬤

1. besides 表示"除……之外(还有……)",它常用在含有 also, another, more, other, else, too 等词的句子中。besides 引起的句子可以放在句首或句末,后接名词、代词、动名词或动词原形及 what 从句等。

   e. g. Besides his father, his mother also went swimming.

     What else did you do besides writing the business letter?

同义词:besides 与 except, but 等做介词时都可翻译为"除了",但其含义有一定的区别。

(1) except "除了……之外(不再有)",着重强调在同类事物或人中除去一个或几个特殊的,表示的是一种排除的关系,有"不包括"的含义。它常与 all, every, everyone, everything, any, anywhere, no, nobody, nowhere, none, nothing 等词连用。except 引起的句子通常置于句末,后面可跟名词、代词、副词、介词短语、动词不定式、动名词、that 从句及 wh-等引导的句子。

   e. g. We all attended the conference except Li Ming.

     I usually go to office by bike except when it rains.

(2) but "除……外,其余都或都不……",它的用法与 except 基本相同,都表示除去的概念,通常置于句末,强调整句的内容,它习惯用于 every, any, all, everybody, anything, anywhere, nobody, no, none 及 who, what, where 等词之后,其后可接名词、代词、形容词和动词不定式等。

   e. g. There is no one here but Mr. Smith.

     Who but a bad guy would do such a thing?

2. 4S shop　4S 店是一种按"四位一体"为核心的汽车特许经营模式。4S 是 4 个 S 开头的英文单词的缩写，即 sale（指整车销售）、spare part（零配件）、service（售后服务）、survey（调查、信息反馈等）。

3. All the prices in the lists are subject to our final confirmation. 价格单中所有的价格须经我方最后确认。此句是报盘常用语。它是虚盘，报价中提出"须经我方最后确认"的保留条件，它仅表示交易的意向，不具备法律效力，而实盘才具备法律效力。句中 subject to "以……为条件，以……为准，须经"这一短语在商务电文中常用，在句中可做状语或表语，在上面例句中做的是表语。做状语的例句：

   e. g. We make you the following offer, subject to the goods being unsold.
   我们向贵方做出以下报盘，以货物未售出为准。

4. We're prepared to make a reduction of 6% on our quotation if your order is exactly larger enough. 如果贵方订单确实可观，我方乐意将报价降低 6%。

   （1）句型：be prepared to do sth. 表示愿意（乐意）做什么事。prepared 做表语后接不定式。

   （2）句型：reduction 说明减少或降低多少时，后接 of，如上句中 make a reduction of 6%。说明在哪方面减少时，后接 in，如：We make further reduction in price. 我方做进一步（再一次）减价。有时在具体说明哪方面减少时也接 on，如：Would you please make a 2% reduction on the quotation? 请贵方将报价降低 2%，好吗？

Exercises 练习

1. 运用 FAB 陈述法推介产品销售有哪四大效果？
2. 中国进出口商品交易会每年在广州举行几次，起止时间是什么？
3. 什么是 4S 店，其英文含义是什么？

译文答案

发音训练15.1-15.2

发音训练15.3

发音训练15.4

Task 16

Orders and Contracts
订单与合同

学习目标：

    1. 了解订单与合同在国际贸易中的重要性，懂得如何签订订单与合同；

    2. 掌握书写订单与合同的格式、内容及要点，明确合同分类并学会书写正式的合同；

    3. 熟练运用订单与合同中的常用词汇、表达方式、基本句型及结构；

    4. 阅读理解订单与合同的内容。

 Text 课文

    In international trade, the acceptance of an offer or an order usually results in a contract. It is a document of agreement terms made by the buyer and the seller on the basis of their offer and acceptance. The rights and obligations of the parties are definitely stipulated in the contract. In a business negotiation, an offer with engagement or a counter-offer is accepted, the transaction is completed and a contract is concluded. A contract will become a formal legal document binding upon both parties after signed. Once the contract has been signed, both parties must abide by the contract and keep good faith.

    The contract which is generally adopted in international trade is the formal written contract, either a sales contract or a purchase order countersigned by the seller, or a sales confirmation countersigned by the buyer. Yet, the sales contract (or the purchase contract) is more formal than sales confirmation, besides, the formal contract consists of not only such main terms as the name of commodity, specifications, quantity, quality, packing, price, shipment, insurance, inspection, delivery, port of loading and port of destination as well as payment, but also those clauses concerning claim, arbitration and force majeure, etc.

    The terms and conditions of the formal contract are included in the following list.

［国际贸易合同（正式合同）包括如下条款。］

（1）Title of contract（合同标题）.

（2）Preamble that covers the name of both parties, the signing date, place and subject（总则，包括双方名称、签约日期、地点及事由）.

（3）Name of commodity that covers the name of goods and the number of articles（商品名称，含货名和货号）.

（4）Quality that covers the standards and the specifications of product（品质，含产品标准及参数）.

（5）Quantity that covers unit quantity and total quantity（数量，含数量单位及总数）.

（6）Price that covers the currency for payment, unit price and amount（价格，含支付货币、单价和总额）.

（7）Packing that covers packing way, weight (gross weight, net weight), volume (length, depth, height) and packing materials［包装，含包装方法、重量（毛重、净重），包装容量（长、宽、高）和包装材料］.

（8）Shipment and delivery that covers the delivery date, destination and time of shipment（装运和交货，含装运期限、交货时间、地点）.

（9）Insurance that covers the assurer's name, coverage, premium and claim（保险，含投保人姓名、险别、保险金额及索赔）.

（10）Payment that covers the date of payment, terms of payment and every detail relevant to payment（支付，含付款日期、付款条件及与付款相关的事宜）.

（11）Inspection that covers the testing objects, standards, cost and authority（检验，含检验物、标准、费用和检验机关）.

（12）Confidential clause that covers specific item, scope of confidential and confidential measures（保密条款，含详细的项目、保密范围和措施）.

（13）Breach and recession of contract that indicates the regulations and compensation as well as responsibilities for breach and recession of contract（违约、毁约条款，指明该条款的有关规则、赔偿及责任）.

（14）Claim that covers the details for claiming, for example, the principle, the conditions, the documents required and the way of compensation（索赔，含索赔有关细节，如索赔原则、条件、文件要求及赔偿方式）.

（15）Arbitration that indicates scope, place and authority of arbitration as well as the details for arbitration in case of disputes（仲裁，明确仲裁范围、地点和仲裁机构以及仲裁所有的细节事宜来解决发生的纠纷）.

（16）Force majeure that lists the causes, date, place and witness documents of force majeure as well as the settlement ways（不可抗力，列出不可抗力的原因、时间、地点和证明文件以及处理的方法）.

（17）Applicable laws that indicates which laws are applied as the principal laws in case of disputes(适用法律,明确适用的法律,以适用的法律作为解决纠纷的准则)。

(18) Miscellaneous clause that indicates what is unsettled in the previous clause of the contract(其他条款,表明在合同条款中尚未明确的其他事宜)。

(19) Witness clause that is formed by the signatures of the representatives of both the parties and their titles(结尾条款,双方代表签字,包括姓名和职务)。

The following cases are examples of orders and contracts.

Case One

Sales Contract

(Original)　　　　　　　　　　　　　　　　　　Contract No. 06 - 07AS

　　　　　　　　　　　　　　　　　　　　　　　Date: July 5, 2012

　　　　　　　　　　　　　　　　　　　　　　　Signed at Wuhan

Seller: Hubei Happy Trade Company
Address: 816 Hanyang Street, Wuhan, Hubei
Buyer: International (H. K) Co., Ltd.
Address: 518 Hennessy Road, Hong Kong

This contract is made by and between the buyer and the seller. Whereby the buyer agrees to buy and the seller agrees to sell the under-mentioned commodity according to the terms and conditions stipulated below.

(1) Name of commodity and specifications, quantity, unit price, total price and time of shipment.

Article No.	Name of Commodity and Specifications	Quantity(m²)	Unit Price (USD/m²)	Amount (USD)	Time of Shipment
SL 1 – 14	Sea-lily fossil plate 300 mm × 600 mm	180	68.00	12,240.00	Prior to October 31, 2010
SL 15 – 18	400 mm × 700 mm	260	80.00	20,800.00	
SL 48 – 55	600 mm × 900 mm	300	120.00	36,000.00	
Amount and Quantity 3 % more or less allowed		Total Amount		69,040.00 USD	

(2) Loading port and destination: Wuhan to Hong Kong.
(3) Terms of payment:
The buyer shall open an irrevocable and confirmed L/C available by draft at sight, in favour of the seller and to reach the seller 45 days before the stipulated time of

Task 16 Orders and Contracts

shipment. The L/C shall stipulate: __3__ % more or less in amount and quantity is allowed, valid for negotiation in China until the 15th day after the date of final shipment of cargo. Partial shipment and transhipment shall be allowed.

(4) Insurance:

Insurance is to be covered by the seller against All Risks as per the clauses of the People's Insurance Company of China for 110% of the invoice value.

(5) Shipping mark: To be effected by the buyer.

(6) Other conditions:

Any alternations and conditions to the contract shall be valid only if they are made out in writing and signed by both parties. Neither party is entitled to transfer its right and obligation under this contract to a third party before obtaining a written consent from the other party.

(7) This contract shall be effected immediately after the date of signature by the representatives of both parties.

    The Seller (signature)   The Buyer (signature)

Case Two

Place an Order

新加坡K. K. V制造公司向武汉大众汽车制造有限公司柴油机分厂定购S195型和S1100型柴油机零配件。泰国富勒经理写给陈凤莲经理的订货信如下。

Dear Ms. Chen Fenglian,

  Re: Order for diesel engine parts (model S195 and S1100)

Thank you very much for your quotation of May 5. We have discussed the items regarding the above models with our engineers and have decided to place an order for the following:

Model	Part Name	Unit Price (USD/PC)	Quantity (PC)	Amount (USD)
S195	Cylinder Liner	5.80	200	1 160
	Piston	8.10	200	1 620
	Cylinder Cap	0.80	200	160
	Oil Scraper Ring	2.10	100	210
	Compression Ring	2.20	100	220
	Piston Rod	1.50	200	300
	Air Filter	3.50	100	350
	Injector Assembly	5.10	100	510
	Main Bearing	4.20	100	420
	Full Injection Pump Assembly	7.80	200	1 560

续表

Model	Part Name	Unit Price (USD/PC)	Quantity (PC)	Amount (USD)
S1100	Cylinder Liner	6.90	200	1 380
	Piston	9.80	200	1 960
	Cylinder Cap	1.00	200	200
	Oil Scraper Ring	3.20	100	320
	Compression Ring	3.50	100	350
	Piston Rod	2.60	200	520
	Air Filter	4.80	100	480
	Injector Assembly	6.70	100	670
	Main Bearing	5.50	100	550
	Full Injection Pump Assembly	8.90	200	1 780

We place this order on condition that you can guarantee dispatch in time to reach us by the end of June. In view of the amount of this transaction being very small, we are prepared to accept payment by D/P at sight for the value of the goods shipped.

We hope that this trial order will open up broad prospects for business between us.

Best Regards.

Yours sincerely,

Fowler

New Words 生词

1. order [ˈɔːdə] n. 命令;顺序;订单 v. 订货
2. agreement [əˈɡriːmənt] n. 协议;同意,一致
3. obligation [ˌɔbliˈɡeiʃən] n. 义务;职责;债务
4. countersign [ˈkauntəˌsain] n. 口令;连署 v. 确认
5. stipulate [ˈstipjuleit] v. 规定,保证
6. claim [kleim] v. 提出要求;要求,需要 n. 索赔;断言
7. arbitration [ˌɑːbiˈtreiʃən] n. 公断,仲裁
8. coverage [ˈkʌvəridʒ] n. 覆盖范围,保险,保险额
9. valid [ˈvælid] adj. 有效的,有根据的;正当的
10. purchase [ˈpəːtʃəs] n. 购买;vt. 购买;赢得

Task 16　Orders and Contracts

➤ Phrases and Expressions 短语与表达

1. enter into	签订,从事
2. abide by	遵守
3. sales confirmation (S/C)	销售确认书
4. force majeure	不可抗力
5. upon receipt of	收到……后
6. diesel engine	柴油机
7. on condition that	在……条件下
8. draw up	草拟,制订

Text Notes 课文注释

1. stipulate 规定,约定。

在句中做及物动词时,后接名词做宾语,也可接 that 引导的从句,句中要用 must,shall,should 或虚拟语气现在时;在句中做不及物动词时,与 for 连用。

e. g. (1) The contract stipulates that shipment shall be made in October.
合同规定 10 月份装运。

(2) The Sales Confirmation stipulates for shipment during September/October, while your Letter of Credit calls for shipment in October.
销售确认书规定 9/10 月期间装船,而你方信用证却要求 10 月装船。

2. valid 有效的。

e. g. (1) This offer is valid for five days.
此报盘有效期为 5 天。

(2) We have received your order No. 2108, valid for shipment on or before August 6, 2008.
我方已收到贵方第 2108 号订单,装船有效期为 2008 年 8 月 6 日以前。

3. coverage 保险,保险范围和投保额。

e. g. (1) We will arrange coverage on behalf of your company.
我方将代表贵公司办理保险。

(2) We want an insurance policy with a more extensive coverage.
我们需要一份范围较广泛的保险单。

(3) The insurance coverage will be for 110% of the invoice value up to the port of destination.
保额按发票金额的 110% 投保,至目的港为止。

4. on condition that 意为"在……条件下","如果……",在that引导的从句中可以用陈述语气,也可以用should 或虚拟语气现在时。它的同义词是:on the stipulation that, on the understanding that。

e.g. We accept your proposal on condition that your L/C should reach us not later than May 20.

如果贵方信用证不迟于5月20日到达,我方就接受贵方的提议。

Safety Tips 安全提示

订货是外贸业务中的一个重要环节,是买卖双方经过询盘、报价后达成共识的一个重要标志,也是以后双方履行合约的一个新的开端。值得注意的是,国际贸易中的订货不能采用口头或电话方式,必须以文字形成下订单。根据国际惯例,下订单时,买方须按货物金额多少的一定比例向卖方交定金。若买方以后单方面不履行约定或取消订单,定金不予退还;若卖方不履行约定、延误交货或造成损失,买方有权向卖方提出索赔或取消订单。

在实际业务中,买卖双方达成协议后,通常还要制作书面合同,将各自的权利和义务用书面条款方式加以明确,并签字加以确认,这就是书面合同的签订。正式合同包括进口合同(import contract)、出口合同(export contract)、购买合同(purchase contract)和销售合同(sales contract)。其内容包括商品名称、品质、规格、单价、包装、装运港和目的港、交货期、付款方式、保险、运输方式、商品检验、索赔、仲裁、不可抗力等条款。

Exercises 练习

1. 国际贸易中如何下订单?
2. 国际贸易的正式合同包括哪些条款?

译文答案

发音训练

Task 17

Automobile E-commerce
汽车电子商务

学习目标：
1. 掌握汽车电子商务相关知识，熟悉其专业词汇及习惯用语；
2. 学习在网上购买汽车的方法。

 Text 课文

 Purchasing Autos Online

Internet technology is more and more developed, and electronic commerce is generally accepted by people. This sales method can expand the scope of transactions, shorten transaction time, save transaction costs, and significantly improve transaction efficiency. Automobile brand manufacturers realize information communication and sharing via e-commerce among suppliers, retailers and departments within the enterprise, so that each link of the supply chain can respond quickly to changes in customer demand and meet customer demand to the greatest extent.

With the gradual transformation of automobile from seller's market to buyer's market, the traditional automobile marketing mode has been challenged by the barrier-free communication mode brought by the Internet. In the increasingly fierce competition in the automobile market, traditional selling methods alone can't meet the current needs. Therefore, as a brand-new sales mode, automobile online sales came into being.

Let's learn about buying cars online and e-commerce through the following dialogue.

In this conversation, Jim is talking with his good friend Tom about the development of car e-commerce and the experience of buying cars online.

Jim: Hey, Tom. I came across a new word e-commerce when I browsed the Internet this morning. Have you ever heard of it?

Tom: Yes. E-commerce means electronic commerce. On the Internet, people like to use just one letter to represent something.

Jim: That's interesting. So tell me more about e-commerce.

Tom: Yes. E-commerce is very popular now all over the world. Consumers are used to buying a variety of merchandise online from such popular Web sites as E-Bay and Amazon. com. And that means buying and selling things for businesses and consumers on the Internet.

Jim: Really? Buying and selling things online?

Tom: That's right. Today, we can even buy autos online. Evidence suggests many customers would like to click their way through vehicle sales as well. Two out of three consumers say a start-to-finish Internet car sale appeals to them, according to survey data from Auto Nation Inc.

Jim: That's great. I just want to buy a new car. Can you tell me more about it? Maybe I will purchase a car online.

Tom: Sure. You can buy a car at an auto dealer's web site, but for some technical and financial reasons, you can't complete all steps online. However the data from the sites can help you decide on make, model and price, because most sites let customers complete credit applications, schedule sales and service appointments and visit automakers' web pages (Figure 17-1 and Figure 17-2).

Figure 17-1　Buying cars online

Task 17　Automobile E-commerce　149

Figure 17 – 2　Visit automakers' web pages

New Words 生词

1. transformation [ˌtrænsfəˈmeɪʃ(ə)n] n. 转换,改变
2. mode [məʊd] n. 方式
3. communication [kəmjuːnɪˈkeɪʃ(ə)n] n. 沟通,传播,通信
4. transaction [trænˈzækʃ(ə)n] n. 交易
5. manufacturer [ˌmænjʊˈfæktʃ(ə)rə(r)] n. 制造商
6. purchase [ˈpɜːtʃəs] v. 购买
7. e-commerce [ˈiːkɒmɜːs] n. 电子商务
8. schedule [ˈʃedjuːl] n. 时间表,日程;计划　v. 预定;安排;编制目录

Phrases and Expressions 短语与表达

1. browse the Internet　　　　　浏览因特网
2. auto dealer　　　　　　　　　汽车经销商
3. credit application　　　　　　信贷申请
4. come across　　　　　　　　偶然遇到
5. service appointment　　　　　服务预约
6. barrier-free　　　　　　　　　无障碍
7. automobile market　　　　　　汽车市场
8. fierce competition　　　　　　激烈的竞争
9. traditional selling method　　　传统的销售方法
10. customer demand　　　　　　顾客需求
11. Auto Nation Inc.　　　　　　AN 公司(美国最大的汽车零售公司)

| 12. E-Bay | 电子湾、易贝(一个可让全球民众上网买卖物品的线上拍卖及购物网站) |
| 13. Amazon | 亚马逊网站(美国最大的一家网络电子商务公司) |

Text Notes 课文注释

1. With the gradual transformation of automobile from seller's market to buyer's market, the traditional automobile marketing mode has been challenged by the barrier-free communication mode brought by the Internet.
   随着汽车从卖方市场向买方市场的逐步转变,传统的汽车营销模式受到了互联网带来的无障碍交流模式的挑战。

2. This sales method can expand the scope of transactions, shorten transaction time, save transaction costs, and significantly improve transaction efficiency.
   这种销售方式可以扩大交易范围,缩短交易时间,节约交易成本,显著提高交易效率。

Exercises 练习

Part I Match the items in the following two columns.

1. electronic commerce   a. 汽车市场
2. browse the Internet   b. 计划购买量
3. sales method   c. 浏览互联网
4. automobile market   d. 信用申请
5. credit applications   e. 电子商务
6. supply chain   f. 服务预约
7. service appointment   g. 供应链
8. schedule sales   h. 销售方法

Part II Translate the following sentences into Chinese or English.

1. Automobile brand manufacturers realize information communication and sharing among suppliers, retailers and departments within the enterprise through e-commerce, so that each link of the supply chain can respond quickly to changes in customer demand and meet customer demand to the greatest extent.

2. In the increasingly fierce competition in the automobile market, traditional selling methods alone can't meet the current needs.

3. E-commerce is very popular now all over the world. Consumers are used to buying a

variety of merchandise online from such popular Web sites as e-Bay and Amazon.
4. 有证据显示,许多消费者也愿意通过浏览网站来购买汽车。
5. 可是网站的数据可以帮助你分析车型配置和价格从而帮你决定购车,因为大多数网站允许客户完成信用申请、销售安排和服务预约,并访问汽车制造商的网页。

译文答案

发音训练

Task 18

Auto Insurance
汽车保险

学习目标：
1. 掌握汽车保险相关的英文术语和词汇；
2. 了解汽车保险的类别；
3. 能够说明交强险的责任范围和赔偿限额；
4. 掌握汽车商业险的主险类型，并说明其责任范围；
5. 了解汽车商业险的附加险。

Text 课文

Auto insurance is a contract that protects your financial security in case of an accident. It is a contract between you and your insurer, specifying each party's rights and obligations. Essentially, your insurer promises to provide specific coverage for you. In return, you pay a premium.

It is mandated by law, the purchase of compulsory traffic accident liability insurance is a requirement in China. Aside from allowing you to drive legally, compulsory traffic accident liability insurance, more importantly, pays for the bodily injury and property damage your car does to the other parties involved in the accident. Compulsory traffic accident liability insurance (CTAI) policy carries liability limits of ￥110,000/10,000/2000 in an at-fault accident. That stands for ￥110,000 in death and disability coverage per accident, ￥10,000 in medical coverage per accident, and ￥2,000 in property-damage coverage per accident. When an accident is your fault, the policy carries liability limits of ￥11,000/1,000/100.

Regardless of the law, having good auto insurance is practical for the driver who wishes to avoid lawsuits or immense repair bills. Compulsory traffic accident liability insurance is generally understood to be the bare minimum level of coverage needed to operate a vehicle. If you cause a serious accident, it may not cover you adequately.

Task 18　Auto Insurance

　　That's why it's a good idea to buy commercial car insurances including own damage insurance, motor vehicle third party liability insurance (MTPL), passenger liability insurance, robbery and theft Insurance and additional insurances.

　　The first four commercial insurances are called basic insurances. If you cause an accident, own damage insurance will pay to repair your vehicle. Own damage insurance will also pay for damages to your car that weren't caused by an accident such as natural disasters. If you were not at fault, the other party's liability coverage would pay for the damages of your car. Third party liability protection for injury or damage insured drivers may cause injury or damage to others or their property at-fault. With MTPL, your provider will reimburse the aggrieved parties for their medical expenses, repair costs, and so forth. Your insurer will pay up to the coverage limits you have selected. Passenger liability insurance is provided to protect the owners and drivers of the vehicle for any legal liability to their passengers in the insured vehicle whether moving or stationary. Theft of cars is not as unusual as some people may think, so for the vast majority of drivers the cost of robbery and theft insurance is well-worth. If the whole vehicle is stolen or robbed, and has not been found for 60 days after the case is put on record and verified by the police criminal investigation, the insurance company would pay for it in full.

　　Once you've selected one or more basic insurances, it's time to consider possible additional risks options, such as glass breakage insurance, additional equipment damage insurance, scratch insurance, waiver of deductible insurance, etc. No additional insurance can be purchased independently, because additional risks only act as supplements to main insurances. The benefits are different with coverage you choose.

　　Let's learn about car insurance by the following dialogue.

　　Mr. Li：Mike, I'd like to have a talk with you over the question of car insurance, if you don't mind.

　　Mike：No, not at all. Go ahead, please.

　　Mr. Li：What kind of car insurance is PICC able to provide for me?

　　Mike：PICC can provide compulsory traffic accident liability insurance, own damage insurance, motor vehicle third party liability insurance (MTPL), passenger liability insurance, robbery and theft insurance and additional insurances.

　　Mr. Li：If I want to insure for repair of my vehicle in an accident, what kind of insurance should I buy?

　　Mike：I suggest you covering own damage (OD) insurance, and the coverage is written in the basic policy.

　　Mr. Li：OK, I see. How long is the period from the commencement to termination of insurance?

Mike：The insurance liability period is one year.

Mr. Li：That's understood. What other kinds of insurance do you suggest I buy?

Mike：I suggest you covering motor vehicle third party liability insurance (MTPL) and passenger liability insurance. You can choose whether to buy robbery and theft Insurance and additional insurances or not according to your needs.

Mr. Li：I'll think it over. Thanks for your help!

Mike：You're welcome.

New Words 生词

1. Insurance [ɪnˈʃʊər(ə)ns] n. 保险
2. accident [ˈæksɪdənt] n. 事故；意外
3. insurer [ɪnˈʃʊərə] n. 保险公司；承保人
4. coverage [ˈkʌv(ə)rɪdʒ] n. 保险范围
5. premium [ˈpriːmɪəm] n. 保险费
6. liability [laɪəˈbɪlɪti] n. 责任；债务
7. compulsory [kəmˈpʌlsəri] adj. 义务的；必修的；被强制的
8. policy [ˈpɒlɪsi] n. 政策，方针；保险单
9. commercial [kəˈmɜːʃ(ə)l] adj. 商业的；营利的
10. additional [əˈdɪʃ(ə)n(ə)l] adj. 附加的，额外的
11. limit [ˈlɪmɪt] n. 限制；限度；界线
12. stationary [ˈsteɪʃ(ə)n(ə)ri] adj. 固定的；静止的
13. theft [θeft] n. 盗窃；偷；赃物
14. independently [ˌɪndɪˈpend(ə)ntli] adv. 独立地；自立地
15. supplement [ˈsʌplɪm(ə)nt] n. vt. 增补，补充
16. commencement [kəˈmensmənt] n. 开始，发端
17. termination [ˌtɜːmɪˈneɪʃn] n. 结束，终止
18. period [ˈpɪərɪəd] n. 周期，期间；时期；一段时间

➡ Phrases and Expressions 短语与表达

1. auto insurance	车险
2. compulsory traffic accident liability insurance	交强险
3. commercial insurance	商业保险
4. basic insurance	主险
5. additional insurance	附加险

Task 18 Auto Insurance

6. own damage (OD) insurance　　　车辆损失险
7. theft and robbery insurance　　　全车盗抢险
8. third party liability (TPL) insurance　　　第三者责任险
9. passenger liability insurance　　　车上人员责任险
10. glass breakage insurance　　　玻璃单独破碎险
11. additional equipment damage insurance　　　新增设备损失险
12. scratch insurance　　　划痕险
13. waiver of deductible insurance　　　不计免赔特约险
14. traffic accident　　　交通事故
15. property damage　　　财产损失
16. bodily injury　　　人身伤害
17. liability limit　　　责任限额
18. minimum level　　　最低限度
19. in full　　　全部；全额
20. PICC (People's Insurance Company of China)　　　中国人民财产保险股份有限公司

Text Notes 课文注释

1. Insurer: The insurance company that has concluded an insurance contract with an applicant and is liable for compensation or payment of insurance benefits.
保险人/承保人：指与投保人订立保险合同，并承担赔偿或者给付保险金责任的保险公司。

2. The insured: The person whose property or person is protected by the insurance contract.
被保险人：指其财产或者人身受保险合同保障的人。

3. Policy holder (投保人): The person that concludes insurance contract with the insurer and has obligation to pay insurance premium according to insurance contract.
投保人：与保险人订立保险合同并按照保险合同负有支付保险费义务的人。

4. Auto insurance is a contract that protects your financial security in case of an accident.
句中 that 引导的从句作为 contract 的后置定语，在翻译成中文时要注意定语前置。所以全句可翻译为：汽车保险是一份能在发生意外时保护你免受损失的合同。

5. No additional insurance can be purchased independently, because additional risks only act as supplements to main insurances.
附加险不能单独投保，因为它们作为主险的补充。

6. What kind of car insurance is PICC able to provide for me?

   中国人保可以承保哪些车险?

7. How long is the period from the commencement to termination of insurance?

   保险的起止期限是多长呢?

Exercises 练习

Part I   Choose the best answer from the following choices according to the text.

1. Compulsory traffic accident liability insurance is generally understood to be the bare _____ level of coverage needed to operate a vehicle.

   A. minimum   B. maximum   C. medium   D. feasible

2. If the whole vehicle is stolen or robbed, and has not been found for _____ days after the case is put on record and verified by the police criminal investigation, the insurance company would pay for it in full.

   A. 30   B. 60   C. 90   D. 120

3. _____ additional insurance can be purchased independently, because additional risks only act as supplements to main insurances.

   A. All   B. No   C. One   D. Two

4. If I want to insure for repair of my vehicle in an accident, what kind of insurance should I buy?

   A. OD insurance.   B. TPL.
   C. Commercial insurance.   D. Additional insurance.

5. How long is the period from the commencement to termination of insurance?

   A. One day.   B. One month.   C. Half year.   D. One year.

Part II   Translate the following into Chinese.

1. basic insurance
2. own damage (OD) insurance
3. waiver of deductible insurance
4. traffic accident
5. minimum level

Part III   Translate the following into English.

1. 交强险   6. 车上人员责任险
2. 商业保险   7. 财产损失
3. 附加险   8. 人身伤害
4. 全车盗抢险   9. 责任限额
5. 第三者责任险   10. 全额

Task 18 Auto Insurance

Part IV Decide whether the following statements are true（T）or false（F） according to the text.

1. (   ) Auto insurance is a contract that protects your financial security in case of an accident.
2. (   ) It is a mandatory requirement and each individual car must be insured, otherwise, the vehicle will not be considered legal.
3. (   ) The primary use of TPL is to provide protection against your physical damage or bodily injuring case of an accident.
4. (   ) Own damage insurance may also pay for damages to your car that weren't caused by an accident such as natural disasters.
5. (   ) Additional insurance can be purchased independently.

Part V Match the items listed in the following two columns.

（1）auto insurance   a 投保人
（2）insurer   b 保险单
（3）commercial insurance   c 商业保险
（4）basic insurance   d 第三者责任险
（5）additional insurance   e 主险
（6）OD insurance   f 承保人
（7）theft and robbery insurance   g 附加险
（8）TPL   h 车险
（9）policy holder   i 车辆损失险
（10）policy   j 全车盗抢险

Part VI Translate the following sentences into Chinese.

1. If the whole vehicle is stolen or robbed, and has not been found for two months after the case is put on record and verified by the police criminal investigation, the insurance company would pay for it.
2. The primary function of the third party liability insurance is to protect the benefit of the third party who is injured in the accidents.
3. Most well-known insurance carriers are considered to be financially more reliable.

译文答案

发音训练

Part III

Auto Beauty and Decoration
汽车美容与装饰篇

Task 19

Auto Body
汽车车身

学习目标：
1. 熟悉车身板件的英文名称；
2. 能用英文标注车身主要板件。

 Text 课文

The vehicle body provides a protective outer hull or "skin" around the outside of an automobile. The body is an attractive, colorful covering over the other parts. Body parts may also contribute to the structural integrity (safety and strength) of the vehicle.

The vehicle body can be made from steel, aluminum, fiberglass, plastic, or composite. The body is normally painted to give the vehicle its appealing, shiny color and appearance (Figure 19-1).

Figure 19-1　Painted body

Today's vehicles are manufactured by using both unibody (Figure 19-2) and body-over-frame constructions (Figure 19-3).

Figure 19-2 Unibody construction

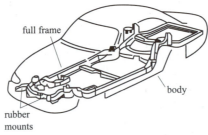

Figure 19-3 Body-over-frame construction(1)

Body-over-frame

The body-over-frame construction has separate body structure bolted to a thick steel framework. The engine and other major assemblies forming the chassis are mounted on the frame (Figure 19-4).

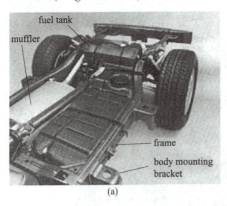
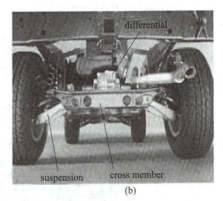

Figure 19-4 Body-over-frame construction(2)

Unibody

The unibody construction uses body parts welded or glued together to form an

Task 19　Auto Body

integral frame. The body structure is designed to secure other chassis parts. No separate heavy-gauge steel frame under the body is needed.

Unibody construction is a totally different concept in vehicle design that requires more complex assembly techniques, new materials, and a completely different approach to repair. In unibody designs, heavy-gauge, cold-rolled steels have been replaced with lighter, thinner, high-strength steel or aluminum alloys. This requires new handling, straightening and welding techniques.

1. Major Body Sections

For simplicity and helping communication in auto body repair, a vehicle is commonly divided into three body sections—front, center, and rear (Figure 19 – 5). You should understand how these sections are constructed and which parts are included in each.

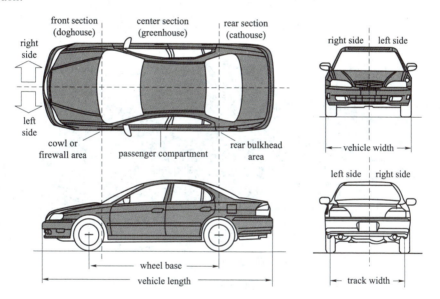

Figure 19 – 5　Major body sections

2. Body Panels

A panel is a steel or plastic sheet stamped or molded into a body part. The major outer panels of a vehicle are shown in Figure 19 – 6. Study the names and locations of each part or panel carefully.

To become a competent collision repair technician, it is important that you be able to quickly locate and identify the major panels of a motor vehicle (Figure 19 – 7 and Figure 19 – 8).

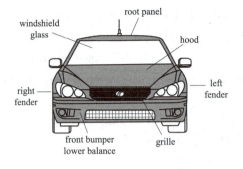
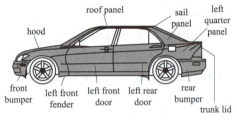

Figure 19 – 6　The major outer panels

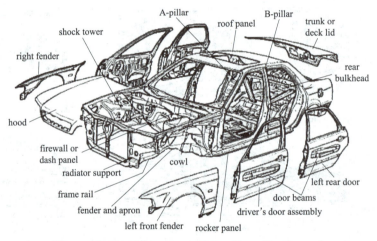

Figure 19 – 7　The names and locations of each panel

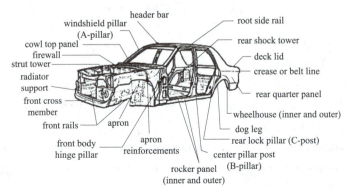

Figure 19 – 8　The names and locations of each part

Task 19　Auto Body

New Words 生词

1. attractive [əˈtræktiv] adj. 吸引人的;有魅力的;引人注目的
2. integrity [inˈtegrəti] n. 完整;完整性
3. fiberglass [ˈfaibəɡlɑːs] n. 玻璃纤维;玻璃钢
4. composite [ˈkɔmpəzit] n. 复合材料
5. unibody [ˈjuːniˈbɔdi] n. 承载式车身,整体式
6. frame [freim] n. 框架;车架
7. assembly [əˈsembli] n. 装配;集会,集合
8. bracket [ˈbrækit] n. 支架;凸出的托架
9. secure [siˈkjuə] v. 保护　adj. 安全的;有把握的
10. section [ˈsekʃən] n. 截面,型材 v. 把……做成截面
11. cowl [kaul] n. 整流罩,隔板
12. firewall [ˈfaiəwɔːl] n. 防火墙,防护　v. 用作防火墙
13. compartment [kəmˈpɑːtmənt] n. 隔间;区划;卧车上的小客房 v. 划分;分隔
14. bulkhead [ˈbʌlkhed] n. 隔板;防水壁;舱壁
15. panel [ˈpænl] n. 板;仪表板
16. stamp [stæmp] v. 冲压
17. fender [ˈfendə] n. 挡泥板
18. grill [gril] n. 栅格
19. competent [ˈkɔmpitənt] adj. 胜任的;有能力的;能干的
20. technician [tekˈniʃən] n. 技师,技术员
21. locate [ləuˈkeit] v. 位于;找出;查找……的地点
22. apron [ˈeiprən] n. (汽车)裙边

Phrases and Expressions 短语与表达

1. body-over-frame　　　　非承载式车身
2. steel framework　　　　钢构架,钢制车架
3. body mounting bracket　车身安装托架
4. cross member　　　　　横梁,横向构件
5. heavy-gauge　　　　　　沉重的,粗重的
6. approach to　　　　　　通往……的方法
7. cold-rolled steels　　　冷轧钢
8. firewall　　　　　　　　前围板
9. passenger compartment　乘客舱

10. rear bumper	后保险杠;后挡	
11. rear bulkhead	后隔板	
12. wheel base	轴距	
13. track width	轮距	
14. windshield glass	挡风玻璃	
15. roof panel	车身顶盖	
16. hood	发动机罩	
17. right/left fender	右/左翼子板	
18. front bumper	前保险杠	
19. rear bumper	后保险杠	
20. trunk lid	行李舱盖;后备厢盖	
21. quarter panel	后翼子板	
22. sail panel	后立柱,翼板	
23. collision repair	(车身)碰撞修复	
24. A-pillar	A柱	
25. radiator support	散热器支架	
26. fender and apron	挡泥板	
27. rock panel	门槛,踏脚板,门下围板	
28. door beam	车门内横梁	
29. frame rail	车身纵梁	
30. front rail	前边梁	
31. front body hinge pillar	A柱铰链加强板	
32. apron reinforcement	前挡泥板加强撑	
33. center pillar post	B柱	
34. rear lock pillar	C柱	
35. wheelhouse(inner and outer)	轮罩(内外侧部分)	
36. dog leg	中间支撑	
37. crease/belt line	腰线	
38. deck lid	行李舱盖	
39. rear shock tower	(后)悬架固定支座	
40. strut/shock tower	(前)悬架固定支座	
41. header bar	(挡风玻璃框架上)横梁	
42. roof side rail	车顶上边梁	
43. cowl top panel	前围上盖板	

Task 19　Auto Body

Grammar Notes 语法注释

The engine and other major assemblies forming the chassis are mounted on the frame.
句中的"forming the chassis"为现在分词短语,用来进一步说明"major assemblies"的作用。英语中常用现在分词短语"doing…"强调被修饰词的功能用途。

Text Notes 课文注释

1. The vehicle body provides a protective outer hull or "skin" around the outside of an automobile. The body is an attractive, colorful covering over the other parts.
   汽车车身就像一层保护汽车的外壳或"皮肤"包裹着其他部件,色彩丰富且富于魅力。
2. The vehicle body can be made from steel, aluminum, fiberglass, plastic, or composite.
   汽车车身可由钢铁、铝、玻璃钢、塑料及复合材料等多种材料制成。
3. Unibody construction is a totally different concept in vehicle design that requires more complex assembly techniques, new materials, and a completely different approach to repair.
   (与非承载式车身相比)承载式车身在汽车设计上是一个完全不同(全新的)的概念,它要求采用新材料,它的装配技术更加复杂,并且维修工艺也完全不一样。

Safety Tips 安全提示

在维修之前一定要确保你已经充分熟悉车身维修工艺和结构原理,你如果不懂汽车的结构原理和维修方法而贸然行事,不仅会造成很大的浪费,并且很危险,严重的还会造成人身伤害。

Exercises 练习

Part I　Choose the best answers from the following choices according to the text.

1. The vehicle body can _____ steel, aluminum, fiberglass, plastic, or composite.
   A. make　　　　B. be made from　　C. make into　　D. made from
2. Today's vehicles are manufactured by using both _____ and body-over-frame constructions.
   A. unibody　　　B. frame　　　　　C. body　　　　D. rail
3. The body-over-frame construction has _____ body structure bolted to a thick steel framework.
   A. thick　　　　B. many　　　　　C. full　　　　　D. separate

4. In unibody designs, _____, cold-rolled steels have been replaced with lighter, thinner, high-strength steel or aluminum alloys.

   A. big   B. thick   C. heavy-gauge   D. large

Part II   Place the names of the parts in the panes in Chinese.

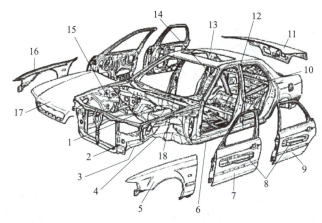

1.	4.	7.	10.	13.	16.
2.	5.	8.	11.	14.	17.
3.	6.	9.	12.	15.	18.

Part III   Vocabulary and structures.

1. What a (wonder) _____ party it was!
2. The film turned out to be (successful) _____ than we had expected.
3. Readers are not allowed (bring) _____ food and drinks into the library at any time.
4. The manager has promised that she will deal with the matter (immediate) _____.
5. We are looking forward to (work) _____ with you in the future.
6. Today e-mail has become an important means of (communicate) _____ in daily life.
7. The visitors were (disappoint) _____ to find the museum closed when they rushed there.
8. Because of the (improve) _____ in the road conditions, accidents dropped recently.
9. When you arrive tomorrow, my secretary (meet) _____ you at the airport.
10. John has worked as a sales manager since he (join) _____ this company in 2002.

译文答案

发音训练

Task 20

Car Care
汽车美容

学习目标：
1. 掌握汽车美容的工艺、设备、工具及材料的专业术语(英文)；
2. 熟悉汽车美容工艺的英文表述方法。

 Text 课文

To keep a car looking like new and clean, we can do: clean car interior; care car body.

 How to Clean Car Interior

Clean interior not just looks great, it's also better for your health. Below are few tips on how to clean the interior of your car.

1. Vacuuming

Remove the floor mats. Vacuum the seats, and the carpet. Using the proper attachment, reach under the seats, around the pedals and the area between the front seats and the central console. Vacuum floor mats separately(Figure 20 – 1).

Use soft brush attachment to vacuum the dashboard and doors(Figure 20 – 2).

Figure 20 – 1　Vacuuming the floor

Figure 20 – 2　Vacuuming the dashboard

Be careful not to damage knobs, vents and sticking parts. Use the same attachment vacuuming the seats.

2. Cleaning Fabric Seats and Door Upholstery

There are a number of upholstery cleaning agents available. Simply spray evenly on the seat or door upholstery and rub vigorously. Then, wipe it thoroughly with a dry cloth (Figure 20 – 3).

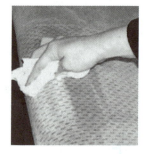

Figure 20 – 3　Cleaning fabric seats

If you don't have an upholstery cleaner, simple laundry detergent will work as well. Just mix some detergent with warm water, dip a clean cloth into it, wring out good and then just wipe the seat. Work hard on dirty areas. Then, rub dry with a clean, soft cloth.

3. Cleaning the Carpet

Clean the carpet the same way you cleaned the seats and upholstery.

Spray evenly with the carpet cleaner and rub vigorously. Then, wipe it thoroughly with a dry cloth (Figure 20 – 4).

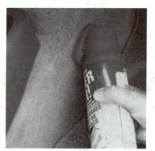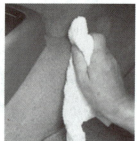

Figure 20 – 4　Cleaning the carpet

The laundry detergent will work on the carpet as well. Damp a rag with a little bit of water and detergent, squeeze the excess of water and rub the carpet vigorously. Then, rub dry with a clean dry cloth.

Task 20　Car Care 　171

4. Cleaning and Polishing the Dashboard

Clean a dashboard, central console, and other plastic parts with a slightly damp cloth. Use very small amount of laundry detergent to remove the stains. Dry with a clean soft dry cloth. To make it shiny, spray plastic polish and spread it evenly with soft brush (Figure 20 – 5).

Figure 20 – 5　Cleaning the central console

Dry-polish gently with clean soft dry cloth. Polish not only makes the dashboard shiny, but also protects the plastic. All you need to do after, is just use a soft duster periodically and your dashboard will look like new for a long time (Figure 20 – 6).

Figure 20 – 6　Dry-polish

5. How to Get Rid of Musty Smell from the Air Conditioner

If you experience that unpleasant musty smell from the vents when the air conditioner is turned on, you can try one odor treatment. It kills the bacteria and removes that mildew smell. You simply spray into outside air intake vent (check directions on the can) (Figure 20 – 7).

Clogged air conditioner drain tube and accumulation of leaves and other debris under the cowl cover also may cause damp mildew smell. Ask the mechanic to check it when you do your next oil change.

Figure 20-7 Getting rid of musty smell

 Car Body Care Tips

To keep a car shiny and protect it from corrosion, please take care of car body.

1. Wash the Car

Wash the car regularly — I'd recommend to do this at least once a month (Figure 20-8). Things like bugs, bird's dropping, or limestone dripping damage the paint leaving permanent stains if not washed off in time. When the car is clean, all the moisture dries up quickly, but when it's dirty, the moisture accumulates in dirty areas causing corrosion. At least once in a while use pressure wash — it removes the dirt difficult to reach. Wash off all the places where the dirt and salt could be accumulated; for example, behind moldings, inside wheel arches, under the bumpers, etc. It's particularly helpful after winter season — to wash out all the salt accumulations that speed up the corrosion process.

Figure 20-8 Washing the car

Task 20   Car Care   *173*

2. Wax the Car

Wax the car regularly (Figure 20 – 9). Wax helps to protect the paint, minimizing harm from chemicals and protecting the paint from fading; plus the car looks shiny. It takes only about 30 minutes to wax a whole car and high quality car wax stays on the car for three to four months. In order to maintain protective coat, any product needs to be reapplied periodically.

Figure 20 – 9   Waxing the car

3. Undercoat and Rustproof the Vehicle

If you live in an area with high humidity, or where the salt use is common in winter months, undercoating and rustproofing your car can be very helpful. Look at the picture (Figure 20 – 10), and this is a part of the brake system located underneath the car. It's completely rusted as you can see. This is only a five-year-old vehicle from a high humidity, coastal area. Sometimes later one of these brake lines can burst and the car will have no brakes.

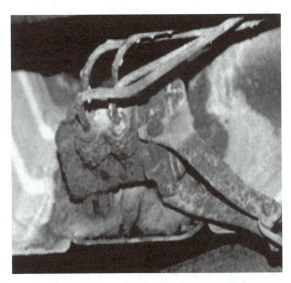

Figure 20 – 10   A brake proportioning valve

Properly-done undercoating and rustproofing can protect important components of the car from corrosion.

4. Repair Stone Chips

The stone chips if not repaired in time will cause corrosion like in this photo (Figure 20 – 11). That's why it's a good idea to repair stone chips as soon as they appear.

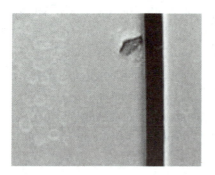

Figure 20 – 11   Stone chips

This one is not corroded yet, so we'll try to repair it. The car is clean and dry and we have all we need — the matching spray paint and a toothpick. If you have a touch-up paint with the brush, you can use it instead, although I found that with a sharp toothpick you can do more accurate job.

After shaking the spray paint very well (for a few minutes), spray very small amount into the cap.

Now, slightly dip the end of the toothpick into the paint in the cap. Very carefully, try to barely fill up the damage with the paint without letting it to come out (Figure 20 – 12).

Now it looks much better and it won't be corroded later (Figure 20 – 13).

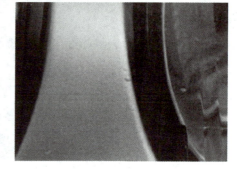

Figure 20 – 12   Fill up the damage with the paint   Figure 20 – 13   Nicer surface

5. How to Remove Residue Marks (Paint) Left by Other Objects

This mark on the bumper was made in the underground parking (Figure

Task 20 Car Care

20 – 14). If you look very closely, it's actually white paint residue over original clearcoat. The clearcoat itself seems to be damaged only slightly. I'll try to remove this mark.

All I need for this is ultra-fine 1900-grit or 2000-grit waterproof sandpaper (the higher number stands for the finest abrasive), polishing compound containing mild abrasive and car wax (Figure 20 – 15).

Figure 20 – 14   Residue marks

Figure 20 – 15   Sandpaper, polishing compound, wax

Very carefully (Don't remove the clearcoat), I sand the marks with wet sandpaper (use only ultra-fine waterproof sandpaper) until all marks are gone (Figure 20 – 16).

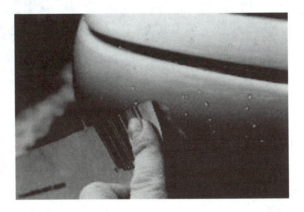

Figure 20 – 16   **Sanding the marks with wet sandpaper**

Now there is no mark, but the clearcoat has lost its shine; I will use polishing compound to restore the shine.

I put small amount of the polishing compound onto the damp sponge and rub well until the clearcoat becomes shiny (Figure 20 – 17).

Last step, I buff the area with the car wax (Figure 20 – 18).

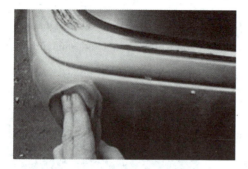

Figure 20 – 17　Rubbing with damp sponge　　　Figure 20 – 18　Ideal look (like new)

6. How to Remove Minor Scratches

Look at the image, these scratches on the trunk were made by the bushes (Figure 20 – 19). It's not a big problem, but I will remove these scratches in two steps: First, I use polishing compound to polish the scratches. It contains mild abrasive and removes very thin coat of painting.

Figure 20 – 19　Minor scratches

I put a little amount of polishing compound onto a damp sponge (Figure 20 – 20) and buff the scratched area in a circular motion until the scratches disappear. But don't overdo it. I'd suggest trying a small area first, to get used to the process. Then I wash off the area completely.

Now it's time to use a liquid wax. I squeeze a little amount of wax onto a sponge (Figure 20 – 21) and spread evenly on the scratched area. I wait a little time allowing product to haze, then, using a soft towel, I buff the wax. You will find an ideal result (Figure 20 – 22).

Task 20　Car Care 　177

Figure 20－20　Putting the polishing compound onto a sponge

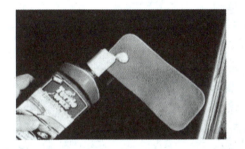 

Figure 20－21　Squeezing the wax onto a sponge　　　Figure 20－22　An ideal result

New Words 生词

1. console [kənˈsəul] n. [计] 控制台
2. vacuum [ˈvækjuəm] n. 真空吸尘器 v. 用真空吸尘器打扫
3. vent [vent] n. 通风孔
4. upholstery [ʌpˈhəulstəri] n. 室内装潢，室内装潢业
5. vigorous [ˈvigərəs] adj. 有力的
6. deterge [diˈtəːdʒ] v. 使清洁
7. detergent [diˈtəːdʒənt] n. 清洁剂，去垢剂
8. rag [ræg] n. 抹布
9. mould [məuld] v. 发霉，铸造
10. polish [ˈpɔliʃ] n. 光泽，上光剂 v. 抛光
11. bacteria [bækˈtiəriə] n. 细菌
12. debris [ˈdebriː,ˈdeib-] n. 碎片，残骸
13. wash [wɔʃ] n. 洗涤，冲洗 v. 洗，洗涤
14. limestone [ˈlaimstəun] n. 石灰石
15. wax [wæks] n. 蜡 v. 上蜡于
16. residue [ˈrezidjuː] n. 残渣
17. abrasive [əˈbreisiv] n. 研磨剂
18. sponge [spʌndʒ] n. 海绵 v. 用

海绵等洗涤、揩拭、擦拭
19. buff [bʌf] n. 麂皮　v. 用麂皮抛光
20. haze [heiz] v. 变朦胧;变模糊
21. trunk [trʌŋk] n. 后备厢
22. clog [klɔg] v. 阻塞
23. cowl [kaul] n. 通风口
24. musty ['mʌsti] adj. 发霉的,有霉味的
25. mildew ['mildjuː] n. 霉,霉菌　v. 发霉;使发霉
26. rust [rʌst] n. 铁锈　v. (使)生锈
27. knob [nɔb] n. 旋钮
28. bug [bʌg] n. 小虫,臭虫

➡ Phrases and Expressions 短语与表达

1. floor mat — 地垫
2. central console — 中控台
3. door upholstery — 车门内衬
4. cleaning agent — 清洗剂
5. odor treatment — 除臭(法)
6. residue mark — 擦痕
7. undercoating — 底盘装甲
8. rustproofing — 防锈
9. waterproof sandpaper — 防水打磨砂纸
10. polishing compound — 抛光剂
11. ultra-fine — 极其细的,非常细微的
12. dry-polish — 擦干并抛光
13. stone chip — 片状破损
14. excess of — 多余的
19. clearcoat — 清漆层
16. wring out — 拧出水来
17. behind molding — 翼子板
18. wheel arch — 挡泥板
19. touch-up paint — 润色漆
20. minor scratch — 细小的划痕

Ⓖrammar Notes 语法注释

How to remove residue marks (paint) left by other objects.
句中的"left"是"leave"的过去分词,过去分词短语 "left by other objects"做定语,

修饰"marks"。

全句可译为:如何清除掉(其他物体在漆面上留下的)擦痕。

Text Notes 课文注释

1. Dry-polish gently with clean soft dry cloth.
   用干净且柔软的干抹布轻轻地将表面擦干并抛光。
2. Just mix some detergent with warm water, dip a clean cloth into it, wring out good and then just wipe the seat.
   将洗涤剂与热水混合好后,拿一块干净的布放进去浸一下,使布刚好能拧得出水,便可拿它来擦拭座椅了。
3. All you need to do after, is just use a soft duster periodically and your dashboard will look like new for a long time.
   此后,你所需要做的事情也就只是用一个柔软的掸子定期掸一下,这样仪表板就可以长期光亮如新。
4. At least once in a while use pressure wash — it removes the dirt difficult to reach.
   偶尔也应用高压清洗机将一些不易够着的地方的污垢冲洗干净。
5. Wax the car regularly. Wax helps to protect the paint, minimizing harm from chemicals and protecting the paint from fading.
   应定期对汽车打蜡。车蜡对漆面起着很好的保护作用,可将化学损害最大限度地减少,并且还可保护漆面不褪色。
6. I wait a little time allowing product to haze, then, using a soft towel, I buff the wax.
   等一会儿,待车蜡变模糊后,用毛巾对其进行抛光处理。

Safety Tips 安全提示

(1) 别对着音响喷水或洗涤剂,应用刷子来刷洗。
(2) 别让水浸透了座椅,否则,不仅会留下污渍,而且会发霉变味。
(3) 真皮座椅很容易划破,小心别让吸尘器的管子划破座椅皮。

Exercises 练习

Part I Choose the best answers from the following choices according to the text.

1. Clean interior not just looks great, it's also better for your _____.
   A. clean   B. health   C. car body   D. face
2. To keep a car _____ like new and clean, we can do: ① clean car interior; ② care car body.
   A. see   B. look   C. seeing   D. looking
3. Use _____ brush attachment to vacuum the dashboard and doors.
   A. soft   B. harder   C. color   D. hard

4. Simply spray cleaning agents _____ on the seat or door upholstery and rub vigorously. Then, wipe it thoroughly with a dry cloth.
   A. fast　　　　B. evenly　　　　C. thickly　　　　D. even

5. Using the proper attachment, reach _____ the seats, around the pedals and the area between the front seats and the central console.
   A. down　　　　B. upon　　　　C. under　　　　D. on

6. _____ not only makes the dashboard shiny, but also protects the plastic.
   A. Cleaning agents　　　　　　B. Water
   C. Detergent　　　　　　　　　D. Polish

7. _____ helps to protect the paint, minimizing harm from chemicals and protecting the paint from fading; plus the car looks shiny.
   A. Washing　　B. Cleaning　　C. Waxing　　D. Undercoating

8. Damp a rag with _____ water and detergent, squeeze the excess of water and rub the carpet vigorously.
   A. a few of　　B. a bit of　　C. a little bit of　　D. a lot of

9. All I need for residue marks over original clear coat is _____ 1500-grit or 2000-grit waterproof sandpaper.
   A. ultra-fine　　B. rough grain　　C. flinty ground　　D. small grain

10. The scratches are not a big problem, but we will remove these scratches in two steps: First, we use polishing compound to _____ the scratches.
    A. clean　　　　B. polish　　　　C. wax　　　　D. wash

Part II　Translate the following into English.
1. 清洁剂　　　　　　　　　2. 抛光
3. 细菌　　　　　　　　　　4. 研磨剂
5. 海绵　　　　　　　　　　6. 车门内衬
7. 冲洗　　　　　　　　　　8. 地垫
9. 真空吸尘器　　　　　　　10. 划痕

Part III　Translate the following into Chinese.
1. cleaning agent　　　　　　2. trunk
3. mildew　　　　　　　　　4. rust
5. vent　　　　　　　　　　6. waterproof sandpaper
7. odor treatment　　　　　　8. wax
9. buff　　　　　　　　　　10. rustproofing
11. central console

Part IV　Translate the following sentences into Chinese.
1. I put small amount of the polishing compound onto the damp sponge and rub well until the clear coat becomes shiny.

Task 20　Car Care

2. After shaking the spray paint very well (for a few minutes), spray very small amount into the cap.
3. Properly-done undercoating and rust proofing can protect important components of the car from corrosion.
4. Wax the car regularly. Wax helps to protect the paint, minimizing harm from chemicals and protecting the paint from fading; plus the car looks shiny.
5. To keep a car shiny and protect it from corrosion, please take care of car body.
6. Dry-polish gently with clean soft dry cloth. Polish not only makes the dashboard shiny, but also protects the plastic.
7. All you need to do after, is just use a soft duster periodically and your dashboard will look like new for a long time.
8. Spray evenly with the carpet cleaner and rub vigorously. Then, wipe it thoroughly with a dry cloth.

Part V　Complete the questions based on the graphs below.

1. Which service is shown in the figure below?

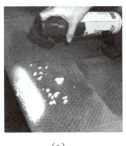
(a)

(b)
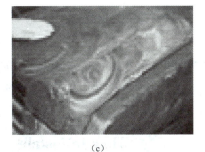
(c)

2. What are there on the table in the figure below?

译文答案

发音训练

Task 21

Automobile Decoration
汽车装饰

学习目标：
1. 掌握汽车装饰的工艺、设备、工具及材料的专业术语（英文）；
2. 熟悉汽车装饰工艺的英文表述方法。

 Text 课文

Making your car stand out from the crowd is not hard to accomplish with all of the different decorations available today. From wheels and tires to music and DVD players, you can customize your ride to your style. Learn how to decorate a ride by following the text.

 How to Install a Sunroof

Just about everyone dreams of driving down scenic roads with the wind in their hair. Of course, this dream isn't always attainable or very practical, but there's always the option to install a sunroof for the next best thing to a true convertible(Figure 21-1 and Figure 21-2).

Figure 21-1　Without a sunroof

Figure 21-2　With a sunroof

Task 21　Automobile Decoration　　　183

(1) The sunroof comes complete with everything that you'll need (except tools) to make quick work of the installation. Before beginning, check the completeness of the sunroof package using the provided parts list (Figure 21-3).

(2) Then, locate, mark and tape the proper position for the roof cutout template (Figure 21-4).

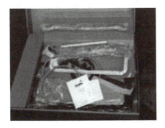

Figure 21-3　Toolkit　　　　　　　　Figure 21-4　Locate, mark and tape the proper position

(3) Position the template flat against the roof and tape it making sure it's straight and there are no creases (Figure 20-5).

(4) Using a single-edge blade, carefully cut out the area of the paper template for the roof cut and draw the cut outline on the roof metal with a marking pen (Figure 21-6).

Figure 21-5　Position the template flat　　　　Figure 21-6　Cut out the area of the paper template

(5) Drill the six holes as marked on the front of the template for the wind deflector, making sure not to damage the inside roof lining.

Note　A "bit stop" can be used for safety (Figure 21-7).

(6) Drill a "pilot hole" for the nibbler (or heavy duty sabre saw) inside the outline on the roof (Figure 21-8 and Figure 21-9).

(7) Using a nibbler or sabre saw, carefully cut out the metal roof along the outline.

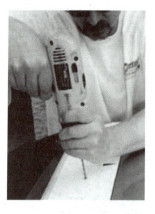

Figure 21-7　Drill the six holes

Figure 21-8　Drill a "pilot hole"

Note: A die grinder can also be used to cut out the metal roof (Figure 21-10).

Figure 21-9　Use a nibbler to cut out the metal roof

Figure 21-10　Use a sabre saw to cut out the metal roof

(8) Carefully peel the roof metal away from the roof ribs and properly discard it (Figure 21-11).

(9) This is what the roof looks like with the metal cut out. No turning back now (Figure 21-12)!

Figure 21-11　Peel the roof metal away

Figure 21-12　The roof with the metal cut out

Task 21　Automobile Decoration　　*185*

(10) Next the roof ribs must be cut out along the edge of the roof metal and removed (Figure 21 – 13).

(11) Unplug and remove the interior light next (Figure 21 – 14).

Figure 21 – 13　Cut out roof ribs

Figure 21 – 14　Unplug and remove the interior light next

(12) Mark the hard headliner using the roof metal as a guide (Figure 21 – 15).

(13) Using a razor knife, carefully cut out the hard headliner to match the roof cutout (Figure 21 – 16).

Figure 21 – 15　Mark the hard headliner

Figure 21 – 16　Cut out the hard headliner

(14) On the inside, lay 3/4-inch tape around the edge of the hard headliner as a guide and cut out the headliner along the outer edge of the tape, thus making the inside headliner cutout 3/4-inch larger than the roof metal cutout (Figure 21 – 17).

(15) Use the die grinder or sabre saw to cut the ribs 3/4-inch smaller than the roof cutout as well (Figure 21 – 18).

Figure 21 – 17　Make the inside headliner cutout

Figure 21 – 18　Cut the ribs

(16) Then grind off the edges of the roof cutout to remove any burrs (Figure 21 – 19).

(17) Apply the protective foil strips, without creases, flush with the cutout edge of the roof, starting with the front strip. Then place the side strips flush with the cutout edge, overlapping with the front edge of the strip that has already been applied (Figure 21 – 20).

Figure 21 – 19 Grind off the edges

Figure 21 – 20 Apply the protective foil strips

(18) Place the wind deflector in the holes drilled earlier (Figure 21 – 21).

(19) Using the special sealing washers and nuts provided, attach the wind deflector but do not tighten the nuts yet (Figure 21 – 22).

Figure 21 – 21 Place the wind deflector

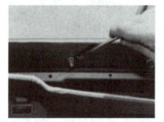

Figure 21 – 22 Attach the wind deflector

(20) Carefully drop the sunroof into the cutout being careful not to dent the roof metal. Also make sure that the sealing rubber is correctly seated on the frame edge as this cannot be corrected after fitting (Figure 21 – 23).

(21) Remove the "A" pillar cap and route sunroof motor wiring down the pillar and under the dash board. Later, you will connect the wires to a verified constant 12-volt source (Figure 21 – 24).

Figure 21 – 23 Drop the sunroof into the cutout

Figure 21 – 24 Remove the "A" pillar cap

Task 21　Automobile Decoration *187*

(22) Remove the two retaining screws from the motor unit on the frame and make sure that the motor can be slid in between the outer roof skin and the inside lining (Figure 21-25 and Figure 21-26).

Caution
　Don't kink the black end tubes for the drive cables.

Figure 21-25　Remove the two retaining screws

Figure 21-26　Make sure that the motor can be slid

(23) Push the front clamp frame part in place and put the motor fastening screws in (Figure 21-27).

(24) Put the rear clamp frame part on and screw in the enclosed nuts onto the stay bolts. Then push the frame sides on. Attach with screws provided all the way around (Figure 21-28).

Figure 21-27　Fasten the screws

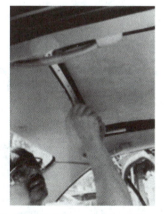

Figure 21-28　Put the rear clamp frame part on

Note
　Do not place any screws into holes with labels stuck on them because the supports for the trim frame are fastened in those holes.

(25) Place the supports in position with the upwardly flanged nose of the support engaging the gap between the mainframe and the clamping frame, attach with the fastening screws and tighten equally (Figure 21 – 29).

(26) Connect the operating switch to the wiring loom and make sure that it works. Close the roof, adjust the wind deflector as needed and tighten the wind deflector nuts (Figure 21 – 30).

Figure 21 – 29 Tighten equally

Figure 21 – 30 Connect the operating switch

(27) Fit the front trim cover, guiding the wire for the operating switch through the opening provided (Figure 21 – 31 and Figure 21 – 32).

Figure 21 – 31 Fit the front trim cover

Figure 21 – 32 Guid the wire for the operating switch

(28) With the roof fully open, fit the side and rear trim covers in place and attach them with the push-in fasteners provided (Figure 21 – 33 and Figure 21 – 34).

Task 21 Automobile Decoration   189

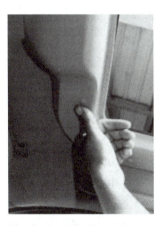

Figure 21 – 33 Attach the covers to the push-in fasteners

Figure 21 – 34 Fit the side and rear trim covers

(29) Beginning in the middle at the rear, attach the edge protection all the way around and trim the excess with wire cutting pliers (Figure 21 – 35).

(30) The finished installation looks almost satisfactory and opens up to let the sunshine in (Figure 21 – 36).

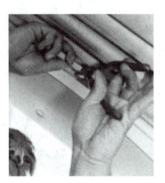

Figure 21 – 35 Trim the excess with wire cutting pliers

Figure 21 – 36 The finished installation

 Replacing Old Carpet

If the carpet in your vehicle has become so worn, damaged, faded or stained that a cleaning or detailing won't do much good, you may want to simply replace the entire carpet. The job may be easier than you think, particularly if you purchase a precontoured replacement carpet made specifically to fit your vehicle.

Materials:

Replacement carpet

Cordless drill with screwdriver attachments

Socket wrench

Steps:

(1) Remove the seats from the vehicle. The seats are held in place by bolts underneath the bench. Use a ratchet wrench to remove the bolts and carefully remove the seats.

(2) Remove the door-sill plates that hold the sides of the carpet in place. You'll also need to remove the seat belts and any other items that are attached to the floor, such as a center console.

(3) With the seats and other items removed, pull the old carpet up from the floorboard and remove it from the passenger compartment. The difficulty of this procedure depends on the vehicle and the type of carpet. Molded, custom-fit carpets do not require glue, so they lift out easily. If the carpet was hand-laid and glued, or if heat has caused the carpet backing to adhere to the floor of the vehicle, it may take more time.

(4) Installation is much easier, if you purchase a molded carpet made specifically for the make and model of your vehicle. For larger vehicles, they may be installed in two pieces. In smaller vehicles, there is usually only a single piece. They already have trim around the edges and padding attached to the underside. They are available in a wide range of colors to match most vehicle interiors. Vehicle carpeting is required to meet certain specifications for flame and ultraviolet resistance.

(5) Before installing your new carpet, take advantage of the opportunity to clean the interior surface of the cab floor. A brush or broom will help with this job. Check the floorboard for leaks or rust spots. If you find rust, you may want to sand the spot and apply a sealer. Leaks should be patched.

(6) Once you've cleaned away any debris from the interior, lay the new carpet in place and position it properly.

(7) Reinstall the seats, center console, seatbelts, doorsills and anything else you removed for the installation.

• Important: Any time that you reinstall seatbelts, it's necessary to torque the bolts to the proper specifications. This is a safety issue, and the torque specs should be in your vehicle's owner's manual or service manual.

Task 21 Automobile Decoration

New Words 生词

1. decorate [ˈdekəreit] v. 装饰，粉刷
2. sunroof [ˈsʌnˌruːf] n. (汽车顶上可开启的)遮阳篷顶，天窗
3. crease [kriːs] n. 折痕，皱褶
4. tape [teip, tep] v. 预留边缘
5. nibbler [ˈniblə] n. 步冲轮廓机，板料切锯机
6. peel [piːl] v. 剥，削，剥落
7. burr [bəː] n. 毛刺
8. flush [flʌʃ] v. 使齐平
9. nut [nʌt] n. 螺母
10. dent [dent] v. 使凹下
11. specifically [spiˈsifikəli] adv. 特定地
12. bolt [bəult] n. 螺栓
13. cab [kæb] n. 驾驶室
14. sand [sænd] v. 喷砂，用砂纸磨平
15. torque [tɔːk] v. 拧(螺钉、螺母等)
16. padding [ˈpædiŋ] n. 填料
17. specs [speks] n. 规格，说明("specification"的缩写)
18. locate [ˈləukeit] vi. 定位
19. mark [maːk] vt./vi. 标记
20. outline [ˈautlain] n. 轮廓线
21. unplug [ˈʌnplʌg] vt. 拆除
22. headliner [ˈhedlainə] n. 顶棚内衬板
23. mainframe [ˈmeinfreim] n. 主框，顶框
24. precontoured [ˈprikəntuəd] adj. 预成型的
25. seatbelt [ˈsiːtbelt] n. 座椅安全带
26. custom-fit [ˈkʌstəmfit] 私人定制
27. screwdrive [ˈskruːdraiv] n. 螺丝刀

➡ Phrases and Expressions 短语与表达

1. stand out from the crowd   与众不同
2. cutout template   剪切模板
3. single-edge blade   单刃刀片
4. inside roof lining   内顶板
5. roof cut   顶棚开口
6. wind deflector   挡风板
7. pilot hole   导向孔
8. sabre saw   电锯
9. die grinder   打磨机
10. roof rib   顶棚加强筋

11. grind off	磨掉
12. razor knife	剃刀
13. foil strip	遮盖带
14. sealing washer	密封垫圈
15. stay bolt	拉杆
16. roof metal	顶棚蒙皮
17. "A" pillar cap	A柱内饰板
18. route wiring	布线
19. retaining screw	固定螺丝钉
20. wire cutting plier	剪线钳
21. trim cover	衬罩
22. clamping frame	边框,侧框
23. flanged nose	法兰凸缘
24. ratchet wrench	棘轮扳手
25. door-sill plate	门槛压板
26. passenger compartment	驾乘舱
27. adhere to	粘贴
28. socket wrench	管钳,套筒扳手
29. wiring loom	接线器,绝缘套筒
30. flame resistance	耐火,阻燃
31. ultraviolet resistance	耐紫外线

Grammar Notes 语法注释

If the carpet in your vehicle has become so worn, damaged faded or stained that a cleaning or detailing won't do much good, you may want to simply replace the entire carpet.

句中的"so...that"是"如此……以致……"的意思,是一个结果状语从句,"so"后面接副词或形容词,对数量或程度进行修饰,"that"后接从句,说明可能导致的结果。例:"The boy is so young that he can't go to school."

全句可译为:如果你车中的地毯已变得如此破旧,并且严重褪色,以至仔细清洁保养很难达到一个好的效果,那么你就该考虑更换整个地毯了。

Text Notes 课文注释

1. Making your car stand out from the crowd is not hard to accomplish with all of the different decorations available today.

Task 21 Automobile Decoration

要想使你的车与众不同并非难事,因为目前有很多种装饰件供你选择。
2. Just about everyone dreams of driving down scenic roads with the wind in their hair.
几乎每个人都梦想驾车驰骋在景色秀美的道路上,微风轻拂秀发。
3. The sunroof comes complete with everything that you'll need (except tools) to make quick work of the installation.
准备好天窗及你将用到的(除工具外的)所有配件,这样可以保证快速完成安装工作。
4. With the roof fully open, fit the side and rear trim covers in place and attach them with the push-in fasteners provided.
将天窗全打开,再安装侧装饰罩和后装饰罩,最后用推入式卡扣将其固定。
5. Beginning in the middle at the rear, attach the edge protection all the way around and trim the excess with wire cutting pliers.
从后边的中间开始,在四周边沿上贴上防护条,最后用剪线钳将多余的部分剪掉。
6. Installation is much easier, if you purchase a molded carpet made specifically for the make and model of your vehicle.
如果你买的是根据你的车的结构而定制的成型地毯的话,安装就非常简单了。

Safety Tips 安全提示

(1) 安装天窗一定要精细,一定要保证滑动机构滑动顺畅和良好的密封效果。

(2) 天窗不仅要安装精细,还要定期保养。进入暴晒季节之前应对密封胶条喷一层橡胶保护剂;进入冬天之前,对机件进行必要的润滑。

(3) 安装地毯时,地毯一定要与地板贴合紧密,在拐弯的地方应裁剪出缺口以缓解张力。

Exercises 练习

Part I Choose the best answers from the following choices according to the text.

1. Before beginning, check the _____ of the sunroof package using the provided parts list.
   A. all   B. completeness   C. tidy   D. number
2. _____ drop the sunroof into the cutout being careful not to dent the roof metal.
   A. Carefully   B. Careful   C. Slowly   D. Orderly
3. Use _____ brush attachment to vacuum the dashboard and doors.
   A. soft   B. harder   C. color   D. hard
4. Making your car _____ from the crowd is not hard to accomplish with all of the different accessories available today.

A. average   B. general   C. stand out   D. evenly

5. Remove the "A" pillar cap and route sunroof motor wiring down the _____ and under the dash board. Later, you will connect the wires to a verified constant 12-volt source.

A. sunroof   B. central console   C. carpet   D. pillar

6. Drill the six holes as marked on the front of the template for the wind deflector, _____ to damage the inside roof lining.

A. making sure not   B. make sure   C. making sure   D. make sure

7. Connect the operating switch to the wiring loom and make sure that it works. Close the roof, adjust the _____ as needed and tighten the wind deflector nuts.

A. wiring loom   B. clamp frame   C. cutout   D. wind deflector

8. Using a _____ or sabre saw carefully cut out the metal roof along the outline. Note: a die grinder can also be used to cut out the metal roof.

A. razor knife   B. nibbler   C. blade   D. lot of

9. Using a single-edge _____, carefully cut out the area of the paper template for the roof cut and draw the cut outline on the roof metal with a marking pen.

A. draw   B. drill   C. blade   D. saw

10. Remove the two retaining screws from the motor unit on the frame and make sure that the motor _____ in between the outer roof skin and the inside lining.

A. can be slid   B. can be fasten   C. fasten   D. slide

Part II   Translate the following into English.

1. 天窗   2. 螺母
3. 螺栓   4. 装饰
5. 挡风板   6. 电动打磨机
7. 密封垫圈   8. A 柱
9. 地毯   10. 褪色

Part III   Translate the following into Chinese.

1. roof rib   2. single-edge blade
3. unplug   4. seatbelt
5. adhere to   6. screwdriver
7. ratchet wrench   8. outline
9. grind off   10. wire cutting plier

Part IV   Translate the following sentences into Chinese.

1. Position the template flat against the roof and tape it making sure it's straight and there

Task 21 Automobile Decoration

are no creases.
2. Carefully drop the sunroof into the cutout being careful not to dent the roof metal.
3. Remove the "A" pillar cap and route sunroof motor wiring down the pillar and under the dash board.
4. The sunroof comes complete with everything that you'll need (except tools) to make quick work of the installation.
5. Making your car stand out from the crowd is not hard to accomplish with all of the different accessories available today.
6. Connect the operating switch to the wiring loom and make sure that it works. Close the roof, adjust the wind deflector as needed and tighten the wind deflector nuts.
7. If the carpet in your vehicle has become so worn, damaged faded or stained that a cleaning or detailing won't do much good, you may want to simply replace the entire carpet.
8. Installation is much easier, if you purchase a molded carpet made specifically for the make and model of your vehicle.

Part V Complete the questions based on the graphs below.
1. What tools does the workman use?

 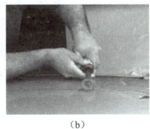 

(a)   (b)   (c)

2. What is the workman doing?

译文答案   发音训练

Part IV

汽车英语电器综合实训篇

一、汽车全车线路实训台介绍

"汽车英语电器综合实训"教学依托为期一周的"汽车整车线路实训"和汽车全车线路实训台而实施,打破常规英语教学模式,将教材中涉及车身电器的某些单元内容打包提取出来,列为"电器实训"这一教学情景,把实训中所用到的实训台运用到专业英语的教学中来,将教室与实训室、理论与实践、课本与实训台有机结合,来完成6个学时的"汽车英语电器综合实训"教学任务,旨在提高学生的感性认识,实现理论知识与实践相结合,推进理实一体化教材和教法的改革。

一、汽车全车线路实训台介绍

(一) 外形结构

外形结构如图1所示。

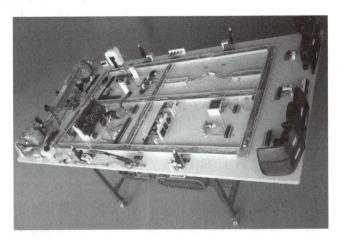

图1 外形结构

(二) 功能

汽车全车线路实训台为终端可插接的实训台,在实训台上面的所有电器部件均采用汽车真实部件(水温、燃油位置传感器除外),学生可参照电路图或维修手册用万用表测量电路的走向和连接;也可将终端用电设备、传感器、开关等断开,对其各种状态下的电阻或通断情况进行测量。

设置故障和排除故障功能:故障设置盒分为故障设置区(预设定为"1"位置)和故障排除区(预设定为"0"位置),两区为对应的并联电路,均设有对应的36个"0/1"开关。设置在"0"位置时,表示断开正常工作的一处电路,而设在"1"位置时,表示接通正常工作的一处电路。利用"0/1"开关,可完成设置故障功能。故障设置完成后,学员可利用专用的仪器或万用电表从面板上检测,检查出设置故障点的位置和内容。

(三) 操作步骤

(1) 在进行台架的实践操作之前,请检查台架电源线(220 V 交流电)是否安全连接,检查可运动部件(如雨刮等)是否能够安全运行。确认无误后,方可进行后续操作。

(2) 将实训台下边蓄电池的开关打开,使刹车灯变亮(实车上制动灯开关为常闭状态,踩下制动踏板,该开关才能打开),把点火开关扭至"ON"位,此时仪表板各种指示灯或仪表应工作正常,如充电指示灯亮、机油压力指示灯闪烁、燃油表和水温表指示可通过调节相应的传感器或模拟旋钮而动作、转速表和车速表指针保持不动等。

(3) 操作台架的灯光照明系统。

① 把前照灯开关开至 1 挡位置:前照灯内的前示宽灯亮,组合尾灯内的后示宽灯亮,牌照灯亮。为仪表板照明提供可调电源,为雾灯照明提供电源。

② 把前照灯开关开至 2 挡位置:前照灯内的前示宽灯亮,组合尾灯内的后示宽灯亮,牌照灯亮。为仪表板照明提供可调电源,为雾灯照明提供电源,经组合开关接通左、右前照灯的远光或近光,若组合开关的变光开关接通前照灯的远光,则仪表板上的远光指示灯亮。

③ 在前照灯开关开至 1 挡或 2 挡时,把雾灯开关打开。雾灯开关开至 1 挡位置,台架前端左、右雾灯亮;雾灯开关开至 2 挡位置,台架前端左、右雾灯亮,左侧组合尾灯内的后雾灯亮。

④ 按下喇叭开关:接通喇叭电路,安装在台架前端的双汽车喇叭鸣响。

⑤ 按下倒车灯开关:接通倒车灯线路,安装在左、右组合尾灯上的倒车灯亮。

⑥ 按下刹车灯开关:接通刹车灯线路,安装在左、右组合尾灯上的刹车灯亮。

⑦ 操作组合开关:将前照灯开关开至 2 挡位置,可完成前照灯的远、近光变光;操作转向灯控制杆,可完成控制左侧或右侧的转向灯闪烁;操作组合开关上的示险开关,可完成控制左侧和右侧的转向灯同时闪烁。

⑧ 操作阅读灯开关:接通阅读灯线路,阅读灯亮。将门控灯打开,按下门控灯开关,门控灯过几秒后会灭(延时功能)。

(4) 操作台架的仪表系统。

① 机油压力指示灯:打开点火开关时,机油压力灯闪烁,表示发动机没有机油压力或机油压力不够;用小螺丝刀顶机油压力低压开关,模拟发动机油道压力,仪表机油压力灯灭。

② 手刹指示灯:安装在台架侧面的制动液罐的液面足够高时,当拉起台架上的手刹开关时,仪表下的驻车指示灯亮起,放下手刹时,指示灯灭。当制动液不足时,仪表下的驻车指示灯也亮。

③ 充电指示灯:打开钥匙开关至"ON"位,充电指示灯亮,将点火开关旋至"起动"位置后,电动机将带动发电机运转,这时充电指示灯灭,表明发动机充电。

④ 水温表:调节水温传感器模拟旋钮,可实现水温表指针的动作,逐渐调高水

温表,水温指示灯会出现从灭到闪烁再到常亮的过程。

⑤ 燃油表:调节水温传感器模拟旋钮,可实现燃油表指针的动作;燃油过低,警告灯也会从亮到灭,或从灭到亮。

⑥ 打开前照灯远光,仪表远光指示灯亮;打开转向灯或示险灯,仪表转向指示灯闪烁。

(5) 操作台架的雨刮清洗系统。

① 操作雨刮系统:把组合开关上的雨刮操纵杆向上摆动到间隔挡,台架上雨刮电动机及联动机构间隔低速运动;把操纵杆向上摆动到低速挡,雨刮电动机及联动机构低速连续运动;把操纵杆向上摆动到高速挡,雨刮电动机及联动机构高速连续运动。

② 操纵清洗系统:把组合开关上的雨刮操纵杆纵向摆动,接通清洗泵及雨刮电路,喷嘴喷水,雨刮电动机低速运动。

(6) 操作台架的中控和防盗系统。

按遥控器上的开锁键和关锁键可实现四门锁电动机及其联动装置的动作。

按锁车键:车门上锁,转向灯闪,喇叭响一声,防盗警示灯闪亮,自动进入静音防盗警戒状态。

按遥控器上的寻车键:喇叭鸣叫 15 s,转向灯同步闪亮,可实现声光寻车。

按遥控器上的静音键:车门上锁,转向灯闪,防盗警示灯闪亮,自动进入静音防盗警戒状态。

按尾门键:遥控开启行李舱(即台架上模拟发光二极管亮)。

触发报警:

在声光警戒中,第一次受到振动触发,转向灯短闪 3 次,喇叭响 3 声;第二次受到振动触发,转向灯闪烁 5 s,喇叭同步报警。若 15 s 内再次受到触发,转向灯亮 30 s,喇叭同步报警,发动机断电止动。

在静音警戒中,第一次受到振动触发,转向灯短闪 3 次,喇叭不报警;第二次受到振动触发,转向灯闪烁 5 s,喇叭不报警。若 15 s 内再次受到触发,转向灯亮 30 s,喇叭不报警,发动机断电止动。

开关触发时,无论在任何警戒状态,转向灯闪亮 30 s,喇叭同步报警,同时发动机断电止动。

按下开锁键,车门开锁,转向灯闪两下,喇叭响两声,可解除防盗。

点火开关打开 15 s 后,按下刹车灯开关,可实现四车门的自动落锁。

(四) 设置、排除故障

设置、排除故障:打开故障设置盒,将里面某一个"0/1"开关(预设为"1"位)扳到"0"的位置,即完成某一处电路的故障设置功能。完成故障设置功能后,打开排除故障盒,将里面对应的"0/1"开关(预设为"0"位)扳到"1"的位置,即完成对该处电路的故障排除功能。

二、各系统部件名称中英文介绍

1. 灯光系统（lighting system）

尾灯总成（tail light assembly）包括：后转向灯（rear turn signal light）、后示宽灯（rear side marker lamp）、刹车灯（brake light）、倒车灯（backup light），如图 2 所示。

图 2　尾灯总成

前照灯总成（headlight assembly）包括：前转向灯（front turn signal light）、前示宽灯（front side marker lamp）、远光灯（high beam）、近光灯（low beam），如图 3 所示。

图 3　前照灯总成

顶灯（dome lamp）和顶灯开关（dome lamp switch）如图 4 所示。
牌照灯（licence plate light）和行李舱灯（trunk light）如图 5 所示。
车身侧面转向灯（side turn signal light）如图 6 所示。

图 4　顶灯和顶灯开关

图 5　牌照灯和行李舱灯

图 6　侧面转向灯

雾灯（fog lamp）如图 7 所示。
闪光器（flasher）如图 8 所示。

图7 雾灯

图8 闪光器

灯光继电器(light relay)如图9所示。

2. 开关控制系统

点火钥匙(ignition key)也称点火开关如图10所示。

图9 灯光继电器

图10 点火钥匙

灯光控制组合开关(light control combination switch)和雨刮控制组合开关(wiper control combination switch)如图11所示。

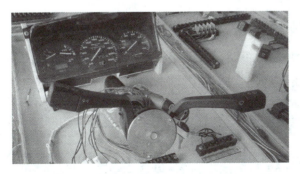

图11 灯光控制组合开关和雨刮控制组合开关

仪表灯光亮度调节旋钮、雾灯开关(fog lamp switch)和警示灯开关(warning light switch)如图12所示。

图 12　仪表灯光亮度调节旋钮、雾灯开关和警示灯开关

喇叭开关(horn switch)、倒车开关(backup switch)和刹车开关(brake pedal switch)如图 13 所示。

点烟器(cigarette lighter)和门控开关(courtesy switch)如图 14 所示。

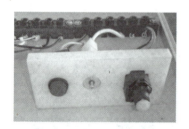

图 13　喇叭开关、倒车开关和刹车开关

图 14　点烟器和门控开关

总电源开关(general power switch)如图 15 所示。

故障设置盒(fault setting box)与故障设置开关(fault setting switch)如图 16 所示。

图 15　总电源开关

图 16　故障设置盒和故障设置开关

手刹杆(hand-brake lever)和刹车踏板开关(brake pedal switch)如图 17 所示。

3. 其他车身电器

熔断器(fuse)与熔断器盒(fuse box)如图 18 所示。

二、各系统部件名称中英文介绍

图17　手刹杆和刹车踏板开关

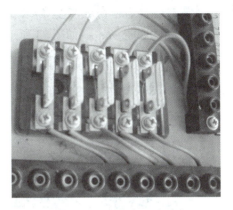

图18　熔断器和熔断器盒

喇叭(horn)包括:报警喇叭(warning horn)、高音喇叭(tweeter)和低音喇叭如图19所示。

雨刮专用继电器(wiper relay)如图20所示。

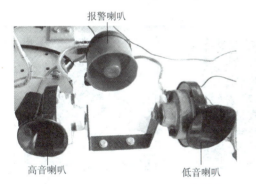

图19　报警喇叭、高音喇叭和低音喇叭

图20　雨刮专用继电器

仪表盘(instrument panel)如图21所示。

图21　仪表盘

起动机(starter)如图22所示。
发电机(generator)如图23所示。

图22　起动机

图23　发电机

制动液报警传感器(brake fluid warning sensor)如图24所示。
制动液存储罐(brake fluid reservoir)如图25所示。

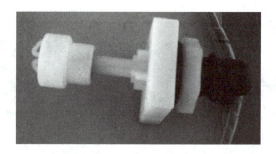

图24　制动液报警传感器

图25　制动液存储罐

蓄电池(battery)如图26所示。
防盗器主机(anti-theft main machine)如图27所示。

图26　蓄电池

图27　防盗器主机

门控指示灯(courtesy light)如图28所示。

燃油量模拟传感器(fuel-quantity simulated sensor)和水温模拟传感器(coolant temperature simulated sensor)如图29所示。

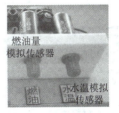

图28　门控指示灯　　　　　　图29　燃油量模拟传感器和水温模拟传感器

车窗玻璃升降器(window regulator)如图30所示。

油量传感器(fuel-quantity sensor)如图31所示。

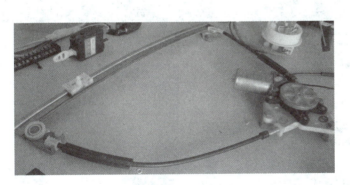

图30　车窗玻璃升降器　　　　　　图31　油量传感器

车钥匙(key)和遥控器(remote controller)如图32所示。

4. 实训常用工具

数字万用表(digital multimeter)如图33所示。

图32　车钥匙和遥控器　　　　　　图33　数字万用表

9V 电池如图 34 所示。

开口扳手(opening wrench)如图 35 所示。

尖嘴钳(nose pliers)如图 36 所示。

螺丝刀(screwdriver)如图 37 所示。

活动扳手(adjustable wrench)如图 38 所示。

绝缘胶布(insulated tape)如图 39 所示。

图 34　9 V 电池

图 35　开口扳手

图 36　尖嘴钳

图 37　螺丝刀

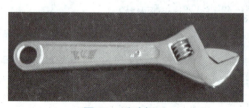

图 38　活动扳手

图 39　绝缘胶布

三、电器综合实训教学组织与案例

在汽车专业英语的教学过程中,我们可以采取电子白板词汇学习游戏法(单词拼写、单词重组、图片与英文词汇匹配、词汇分类识别游戏等)、卡片识别法、看图识词法、圈词训练法、标识学习法、听写词汇法、成果分享法、小组讨论法和复杂句子对比纠错法等多种教学方法。电器综合实训的教学组织主要是运用如图 40 所示的这些电器词汇英文卡片,让学生通过电器实训周前三天的学习与实践,进一步训练将英文卡片与实训台上各处的电器名称相匹配的能力。

图40 汽车电器词汇英文卡片

汽车车身电器英文卡片识别能力测试案例：
（1）在课堂教学中，组织同学们在教室里进行卡片识别训练。
（2）在实训室，按照抽签的顺序，被测试的同学随机领取数枚电器英文卡片。
（3）在规定的1分钟内，将卡片放置于轿车实训台上相应的位置。
（4）放置正确方可得分。有计时员和考评员协助老师进行测试。

这堂电器综合实训课，让轿车实训台既是老师的教具，也是同学们的学具，还成了大家的"玩具"（图41）。

图41 实训情景

图41 实训情景(续)

四、电器实训学习工单

电器实训学习工单1

课程：汽车专业英语	班级：	组别：
学习任务： 1.熟悉汽车仪表系统电路图。 2.熟悉电路图中所对应的英文表达	日期：	得分：
	组员：	

Translate the following Chinese into English.
汽车仪表系统电路图：

（电路图：液面传感器 FU、燃油表、起动开关"ON"、IG、水温传感器、接地 E、水温表、TU、油位报警传感器、油位报警灯、机油压力感应塞、机油报警灯、电脑故障灯接口 W、故障灯、制动液面报警开关、制动灯、燃油滤清器报警开关、滤清器报警灯、充电熔断器、充电指示灯、点火熔断器）

四、电器实训学习工单

电器实训学习工单 2

课程：汽车专业英语	班级：	组别：
	日期：	得分：
学习任务:熟悉两种点火系统零部件名称的中英文表达	组员：	

Translate the following Chinese into English.

(1) 传统点火系统电路图：

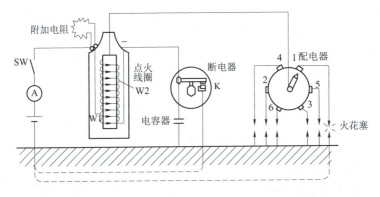

(2) 电子点火系统的电路图：

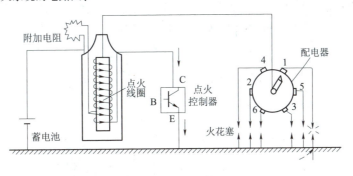

电器实训学习工单 3

课程：汽车专业英语	班级：	组别：
学习任务： 1. 熟悉汽车起动系统电路图。 2. 熟记起动系统专业术语英文表达	日期：	得分：
	组员：	

Translate the following Chinese into English.

起动系统电路图：

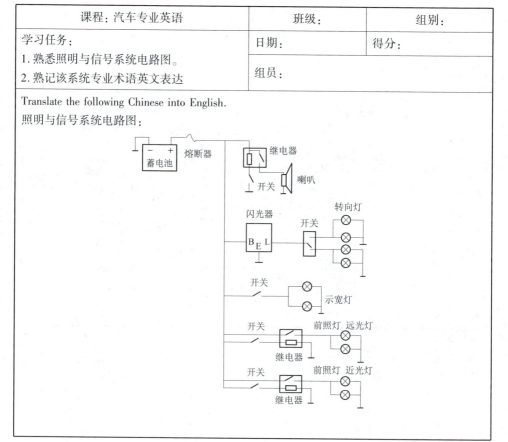

电器实训学习工单 4

课程：汽车专业英语	班级：	组别：
学习任务： 1. 熟悉照明与信号系统电路图。 2. 熟记该系统专业术语英文表达	日期：	得分：
	组员：	

Translate the following Chinese into English.

照明与信号系统电路图：

五、专业词汇拓展训练工单

专业词汇拓展训练工单 1

姓名_____ 学号_____ 序号_____ 分数_____

从下列每小题 4 个选项中,勾选一个与英文单词对应的中文词(满分 100)。

1. Crankshaft　　　　　(凸轴,凸轮轴,曲轴,曲柄轴)
2. Spring　　　　　　　(春天,弹簧,秋天,冬天)
3. Nut　　　　　　　　(坚果,苹果,螺母,螺钉)
4. Bolt　　　　　　　　(螺钉,螺母,孔,螺栓)
5. Park　　　　　　　　(公园,驻车,停车场,位置)
6. Part　　　　　　　　(公园,驻车,零件,部分)
7. Flywheel　　　　　　(飞轮,车轮,轮胎,轮轴)
8. Start　　　　　　　　(开始,起动,火花,明星)
9. Oil　　　　　　　　　(机油,石油,柴油,汽油)
10. Fuel　　　　　　　　(燃油,汽油,柴油,机油)

专业词汇拓展训练工单 2

姓名_____ 学号_____ 序号_____ 分数_____

从下列每小题 4 个选项中,勾选一个与英文单词对应的中文词(满分 100)。

1. Diesel engine　　　　(柴油机,汽油机,内燃机,外燃机)
2. Gasoline engine　　　(柴油机,汽油机,内燃机,外燃机)
3. Cylinder block　　　　(气缸体,气缸套,气缸盖,气缸壁)
4. Cylinder head　　　　(气缸体,气缸套,气缸盖,气缸壁)
5. Cylinder sleeve　　　 (气缸体,气缸套,气缸盖,气缸壁)
6. Cylinder wall　　　　(气缸体,气缸套,气缸盖,气缸壁)
7. Engine　　　　　　　(发动机,电动机,起动机,发电机)
8. Motor　　　　　　　(发动机,电动机,起动机,发电机)
9. Starter　　　　　　　(发动机,电动机,起动机,发电机)
10. Generator　　　　　(发动机,电动机,起动机,发电机)

专业词汇拓展训练工单 3

姓名_____ 学号_____ 序号_____ 分数_____

从下列每小题 4 个选项中,勾选一个与英文单词对应的中文词(满分 100)。

1. Fuel pump　　　　　(燃油泵,机油泵,水泵,液压泵)
2. Oil pump　　　　　　(燃油泵,机油泵,水泵,液压泵)

3. Water pump　　　　　　　(燃油泵,机油泵,水泵,液压泵)

4. Hydraulic pump　　　　　(燃油泵,机油泵,水泵,液压泵)

5. Air filter　　　　　　　(空滤器,机油滤清器,燃油滤清器,柴油滤清器)

6. Oil filter　　　　　　　(空滤器,机油滤清器,燃油滤清器,柴油滤清器)

7. Fuel filter　　　　　　　(空滤器,机油滤清器,燃油滤清器,柴油滤清器)

8. Injector　　　　　　　　(喷油器,增压器,滤清器,冷却器)

9. Radiator　　　　　　　　(喷油器,散热器,滤清器,冷却器)

10. Turbocharger　　　　　(增压器,散热器,滤清器,冷却器)

专业词汇拓展训练工单 4

姓名_____　学号_____　序号_____　分数_____

连线匹配相应的中、英文单词(满分 100)。

1. Start　　　　　　　空挡

2. Park　　　　　　　弹簧

3. Neutral　　　　　　轴承

4. Spring　　　　　　驻车挡

5. Bearing　　　　　　搭铁

6. Nut　　　　　　　断路

7. Ground　　　　　　起动

8. Open　　　　　　　零部件

9. Short　　　　　　　短路

10. Part　　　　　　　螺母

专业词汇拓展训练工单 5

姓名_____　学号_____　序号_____　分数_____

连线匹配相应的中、英文单词(满分 60)。

1. Battery　　　　　　电阻

2. Current　　　　　　电路

3. Voltage　　　　　　电容器

4. Circuit　　　　　　电流

5. Resister　　　　　　蓄电池

6. Condenser　　　　　电压

专业词汇拓展训练工单 6

姓名_____ 学号_____ 序号_____ 分数_____

连线匹配相应的中、英文单词(满分60)。

1. AT—automatic transmission　　　　　　　无级变速箱

2. MT—manual transmission　　　　　　　　手动变速箱

3. CVT—continuously variable transmission　　自动变速箱

4. Screw　　　　　　　　　　　　　　　　螺母

5. Bolt　　　　　　　　　　　　　　　　　螺钉

6. Nut　　　　　　　　　　　　　　　　　螺栓

答案

参 考 文 献

[1] 吴金顺. 汽车专业英语(第2版)[M]. 北京:北京理工大学出版社,2011.

[2] [美]James D. Halderman, Chase D. Mitchell,Jr. 汽车发动机理论与维修[M]. 李克,等,译. 北京:中国劳动社会保障出版社,2006.

[3] 沈彬彬,吴志平. 汽车专业英语[M]. 上海:上海交通大学出版社,2016.

[4] [美]Roy S. Cox. 汽车第二代车载诊断系统(OBD Ⅱ)解析[M]. 冯永忠,译. 北京:机械工业出版社,2007.

[5] 彭安娜. LED汽车前照灯的光学系统设计研究[D]. 广州:华南理工大学,2016.

[6] 自远. LED技术在汽车照明系统中的应用分析[J]. 北京:现代信息科技,2018, 2(06):51-52.

[7] [美]Tom Birch. Automotive Heating and Air Conditioning [M]. Person Education, Inc.,2006.

[8] 中国科学院计算机语言信息工程研究中心. 汉英汽车技术词典[M]. 北京:人民交通出版社,2004.

[9] 汽车技术编辑组. 英汉汽车缩略语词典[M]. 北京:人民交通出版社,2005.

[10] 徐琦. 汽车采购英语[M]. 武汉:武汉大学出版社,2010.

[11] 陈莉. 浅析汽车行业电子商务的发展现状与对策[J]. 内蒙古科技与经济, 2016(1).

[12] 周晓燕. 浅析我国汽车产业的网上销售模式[J]. 市场论坛,2011(5).

[13] [美]James E. Duffy, Robert Scharff. Auto Body Repair Technology[M]. New York,USA:Thomson Learning, Inc.,2004.